key: Bm – bream E – eels
Cp – common carp

The Observer's Pocket Series

COARSE FISHING

The Observer Books

A POCKET REFERENCE SERIES COVERING A WIDE RANGE OF SUBJECTS

NATURAL HISTORY
Birds · Birds' Eggs · Wild Animals · Zoo Animals
Farm Animals · Freshwater Fishes · Sea Fishes
Tropical Fishes · Butterflies · Larger Moths
Caterpillars · Insects · Pond Life · Sea and Seashore
Seashells · Pets · Dogs · Horses and Ponies · Cats
Trees · Wild Flowers · Grasses · Mushrooms
Lichens · Cacti · Garden Flowers · Flowering Shrubs
Vegetables · House Plants · Geology · Rocks and Minerals · Fossils · Weather · Astronomy

SPORT
Soccer · Cricket · Golf · Tennis · Coarse Fishing
Fly Fishing · Show Jumping · Motor Sport

TRANSPORT
Automobiles · Aircraft · Commercial Vehicles
Motorcycles · Steam Locomotives · Ships · Small Craft · Manned Spaceflight · Unmanned Spaceflight

ARCHITECTURE
Architecture · Churches · Cathedrals · Castles

COLLECTING
Awards and Medals · Coins · Firearms · Furniture
Postage Stamps · Glass · Pottery and Porcelain

ARTS AND CRAFTS
Music · Painting · Modern Art · Sewing · Jazz
Big Bands

HISTORY AND GENERAL INTEREST
Ancient Britain · Flags · Heraldry · European Costume

TRAVEL
London · Tourist Atlas GB · Lake District · Cotswolds

The Observer's Book of

COARSE FISHING

PETER WHEAT

LINE DRAWINGS BY BAZ EAST

WITH 8 COLOUR PLATES, 18 BLACK AND WHITE PHOTOGRAPHS AND NUMEROUS DIAGRAMS IN THE TEXT

FREDERICK WARNE

LONDON

Reprinted 1977
Reprinted 1979

Library of Congress Catalog
Card No. 74-21041

ISBN 0 7232 1543 x

Printed in Great Britain by
William Clowes & Sons Limited
Beccles and London
D5829·479

Preface

This is essentially a book about the basics of coarse fishing, and its main purpose is to introduce the reader to the sport and assist him to a stage where he is able to catch fish fairly consistently.

I have endeavoured to cover the important points of the subject as comprehensively as is possible in a book of this size. To give scope for study of specialized aspects a list of books for further reading has been included at the back.

Acknowledgement is due to the following for the illustrations in this book:

Ray Forsberg, Bill Howes, Trevor Hutchings and Barrie Rickards for colour photographs, and to my good friend Baz East for drawings in the text. The black and white photographs are from my own collection.

I must also acknowledge the countless generations of anglers, past and present, who have both directly and indirectly given me my own meagre understanding of this fascinating sport. Of special mention: Francis Francis, Hugh Tempest Sheringham, Richard Walker, Bernard Venables and Fred J. Taylor.

And lastly, grateful thanks to the many friends with whom I have shared pleasantly memorable hours at the waterside. Particularly: Ron Barnett, Bob Church and David Carl Forbes. My enthusiasm has been quickened through fishing days spent in their company.

Peter Wheat

Contents

4: Final Matters

List of Colour Plates

Introduction

The seed of the sport of angling was sown far back in the Old Stone Age when fish hunting was one of man's principal food-gathering methods. Further back than approximately 8,000 BC, the human race really existed little better than the animals. They lived in small family groups, in caves and such like, and they survived under bitterly cold conditions by collecting berries, roots and edible plants, and by hunting animals and fish.

Earliest fishing techniques included spearing with bone harpoons and lances fire-hardened or fitted with flint tips at their business ends, and netting and trapping. Also, though no evidence survives to support it, it is quite feasible that paralyzing herbs were used to drug fish so that they floated to the surface for net collection—a method popular among certain native tribes to this day.

Exactly how important fish-catching was to Old Stone Age groups would largely have depended on the nearness or otherwise of lakes and streams. However, there is evidence to support the view that some family groups were quite prepared to venture many miles from their cave dwellings during the spring and summer in order to station themselves at vantage points along a river, and trap migrating salmon and trout on their journey upstream to the spawning redds. Traces of these prehistoric fishery sites have been found in France, and at New Ferry on the River Bann in Northern Ireland.

That fish were held in the highest esteem by our most ancient ancestors is obvious from the drawings and carvings which have survived on cave walls and antler bones. In France, for example, fish carvings dating to 12,000 BC exist which depict salmon, eel and pike, as well as other more carp-like species.

Perhaps the most remarkable of these piscatorial representations is a low-relief sculpture of a fish 3 ft (90 cm) long cut into the floor of the Grotte du Poisson in central France. Complete with proud dorsal, mouth, fins and gills, it is clearly a migratory species—probably salmon.

Also from France has come another interesting item—an antler stick depicting a shoal of four life-like fish swimming a river between the antlers and legs of two reindeer—a huntin' fishin' symbol if ever there was one.

Experts believe that early man carved and painted animal and fish pictures not solely for pleasure and beautification of his dwellings, but also as part of magical rituals which enabled him to catch them all the better. It makes me wonder if the paintings, photographs and stuffed carcasses which adorn the walls of anglers' dens have rather more primeval significance than mere decoration.

Old Stone Age fishermen went a hunting strictly for food; there was certainly nothing sporting about it. Pleasure fishing—rod, line and hook angling—was a much later development, and came about as a side effect of the Neolithic revolution, which began in south-western Asia—in areas such as Turkey's Anatolian plateau where wheat and barley grew wild, and where the ancestors of cattle, pigs, dogs, sheep and goats roamed abundantly.

Crop cultivation and animal breeding in this area led to a food-producing economy: farming. It was a far more settled way of life, with individual family groups joining together to work and to defend themselves against enemy attack. There was food to spare, more time for leisure activities, and greater security than ever before. It was the birth of civilization and, in my opinion, the birth of angling, too.

Obviously trapping fish for food remained fairly important to Neolithic man—especially in the embryo trial and error days of farming—and harpoons, nets, and traps closely similar to modern osier weels were commonly in use. So too were hooks, lines and crude stick-rods.

Hook materials included flint, thin wooden forks, bird-bone forks, animal bones, and even shells. At Shaheinab in the Sudan, Neolithic fishermen carved their hooks from Nile oyster shells.

Slowly but surely, over a span of several thousand years, the Neolithic stage spread across Europe, eventually reaching the shore of Britain some 5,000 to 6,000 years ago. The first farmers of this country settled in the fertile lands of Hampshire, Dorset and Wiltshire, and it is more than probable that pleasure fishing was enjoyed by them in rivers such as the Hampshire Avon, Dorset Stour, Test and Itchen.

With the growth of agriculture in Britain, hunting and fishing would consequently have become less important in advanced farming communities—fishing for the majority being but amusement to be enjoyed in the quiet hours between tilling fields and feeding domestic stock.

Today, Britain is just one of many countries able to claim angling as its largest participant sport. Adherents number in millions and a significant percentage of them angle fresh water for coarse fish species.

Indigenous sporting species which entered British waters following the close of the last Great Ice Age (about 10,000 years ago) include: roach, dace, rudd, grayling, perch, chub, tench, barbel, eel, bream and pike.

Sporting species introduced later by man include: common carp, crucian carp, catfish and zander.

'There is an indescribable fealty among fishermen greater than among any other group of men. There is devotion to the out-of-doors and relief from the grind of modern life that stamp them at once as men of spirit.'

HERBERT CLARK HOOVER

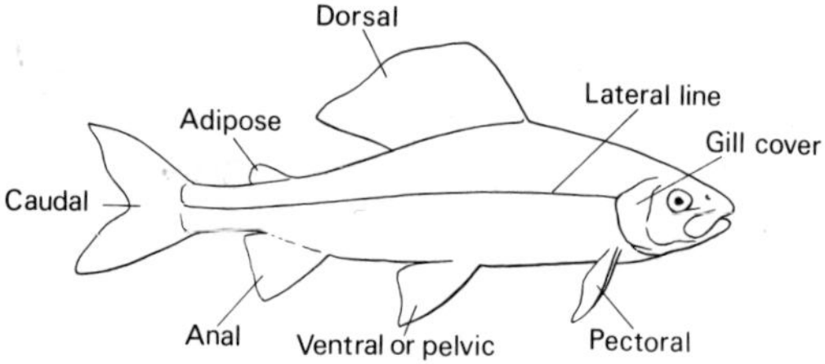

Fins and other external features of a fish

I: FIRST CONSIDERATIONS

Introducing the Quarry

From a wide variety of fishes inhabiting British waters a total of 16 coarse species can be selected as being of outstanding sporting value. Of these by far the best known and most popular is the roach, and therefore it will be appropriate to commence brief descriptions of the coarse angler's quarry with this fine fish.

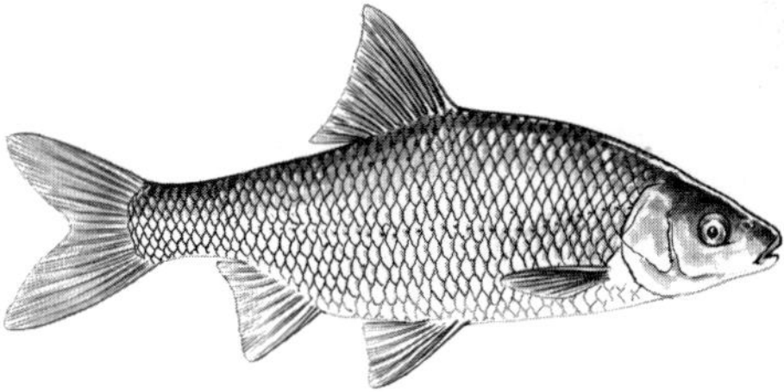

The Roach

Family CYPRINIDAE *Rutilus rutilus*

Identification: A streamlined fish, deepening in the belly and hump-backing slightly as it increases size. The back is greeny brown with hints of metallic blue, flanks silver and underparts ivory white. Dorsal and caudal fins are reddish brown, pectoral fins orange red, and ventral fins coral red. The eyes are either watery red or wine red.

Distribution: Waters of every size and type. Common throughout England apart from Devon and Cornwall where it is rare, southern parts of Scotland and eastern Wales. Localized in Ireland but abounding in such waters as the Cork Blackwater, the Fairy Water near Omagh in Co. Tyrone, and the systems of Foyle and Erne.
Growth: Sizeable at 1 lb (450 g), a specimen at 2 lb (900 g). Although the species is capable of reaching weight in excess of 4 lb (1·8 kg), roach of 3 lb (1·4 kg) plus are rarely caught.

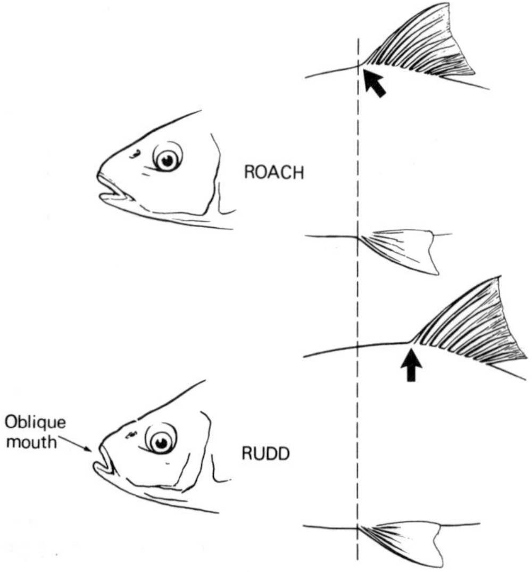

Points of identification between roach and rudd

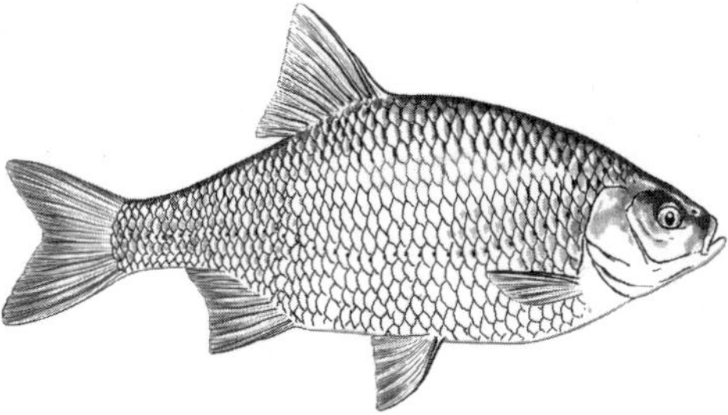

The Rudd

Family CYPRINIDAE *Scardinius erythropthalmus*

Identification: Young rudd and roach are similar both in general shape and colour. They can be easily told apart by mouth shape and dorsal fin position.

The leading edge of the roach dorsal is rooted almost directly above that of the pelvic fins, whilst the rudd dorsal is set much further back towards the tail. The lower lip of the rudd protrudes beyond the upper lip, a feature absent in the roach.

In large rudd the body is deeper for length than that of roach, and the colouring is more distinctive: richly red fins and flanks of golden bronze.

Distribution: Stillwaters, canals and slow rivers. Prolific and large-growing in Ireland, less widely-distributed in England, absent from Scotland. The fens of Cambridgeshire, Norfolk, Lincolnshire and north Somerset, are traditionally fine rudd areas. Elsewhere in England waters where the species achieves notable weight are few and far between.

Growth: At $1\frac{1}{2}$ lb (680 g) a good fish, at 2 lb (900 g) a specimen for English waters, and at $2\frac{1}{2}$ lb (1·1 kg) a specimen for Irish waters. Few rudd weighing 4 lb (1·8 kg) or over have been caught, but nevertheless there is no doubt that 5 lb (2·2 kg) rudd exist —more so in Ireland.

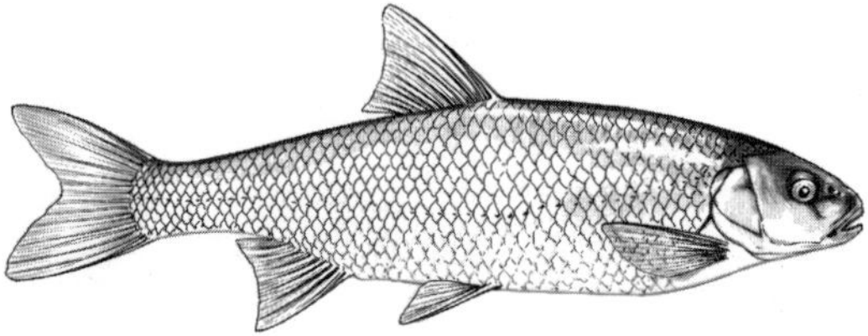

The Dace

Family CYPRINIDAE *Leuciscus leuciscus*

Identification: The dace is a slimly built fish with a greeny brown back, silver flanks and a white belly. The fins are watery, but big dace in some rivers have red, orange or yellow in their pelvic and ventral fins.
Distribution: Rivers and streams. A few lakes also contain them. Widespread in England, absent from Scotland and the western parts of Wales. In Ireland restricted to the Cork Blackwater and the tributaries of this river.
Growth: This is the smallest of the sporting species. A 6 oz (170 g) dace is fair size, at 12 oz (340 g) a specimen. Dace of 1 lb (450 g) or over should be the subject of careful photographic record—if not a glass case.

The Crucian Carp

Family CYPRINIDAE *Carassius carassius*

Identification: A short, deep, chunky-looking fish, with big scales, long high dorsal—convex on the top edge—and a caudal fin only slightly notched, almost spatular. The back is dark amber, the flanks golden bronze, and the underparts yellowy splashed with reddish orange patches.

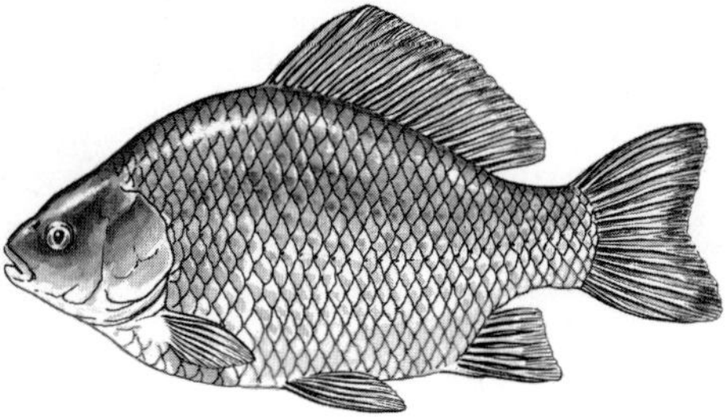

Distribution: Lakes, ponds, pits and slow rivers. Localized in England, southern and eastern parts mainly. Absent from Scotland, Ireland and Wales. *Growth:* Excellent at 1½ lb (680 g). Crucian of 2 lb (900 g) plus are specimens. In a few choice waters live crucian weighing between 3 (1·3) and 5 lb (2·2 kg).

The Common Carp

Family CYPRINIDAE *Cyprinus carpio*
Identification: Wild common carp are long, sleek fish, compared with domestic king carp strains imported from the continent which are short and immensely plump. All common carp possess four barbules—

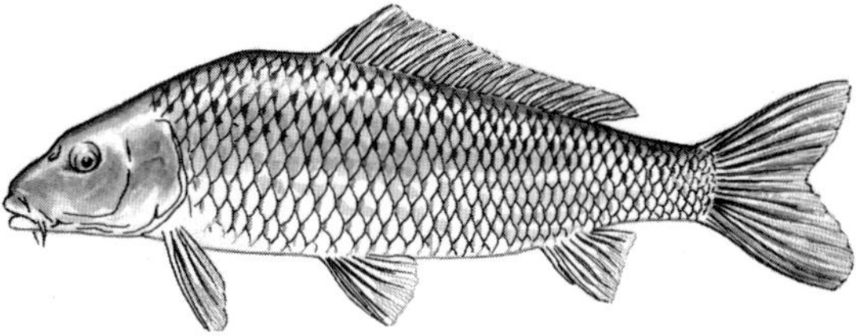

two on each side of the upper lip—and a long concave dorsal fin. The back is blue grey, the flanks brownly golden and the belly orange, yellow or white. Wild carp are always covered with big scales. King carp include, as well as fully-scaled fish, specimens which are partially scaled (mirror carp) and specimens with only two or three scales on each flank or no scales at all (leather carp).

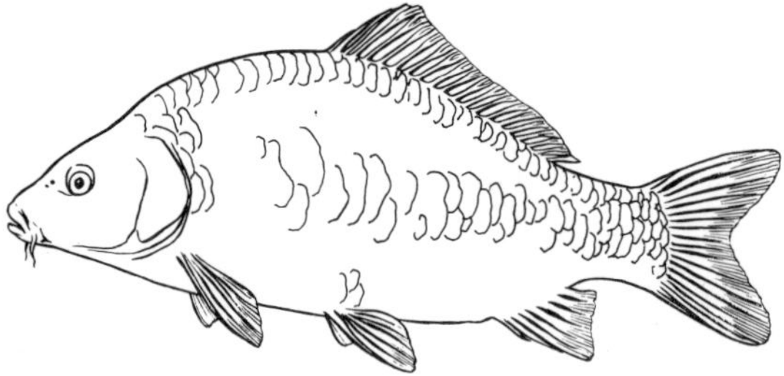

Partially scaled mirror carp

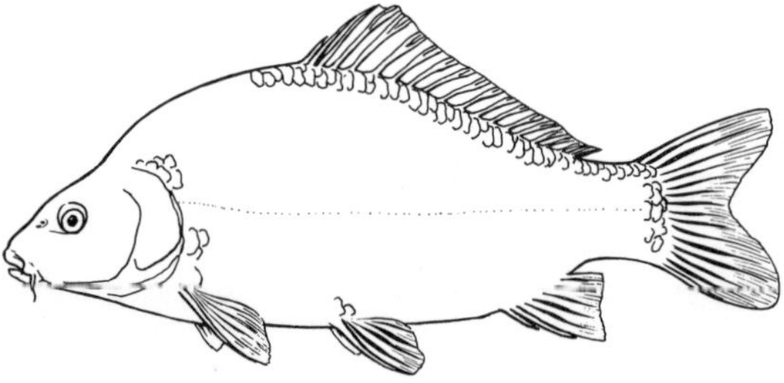

Partially scaled mirror carp

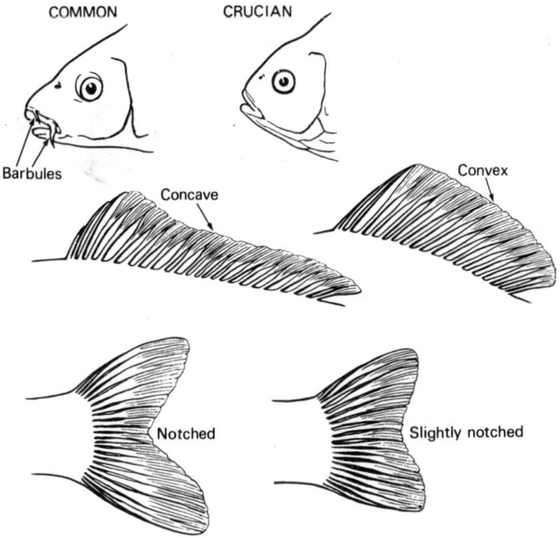

Points of identification between common carp and crucian carp

restricted to along the top of the back and the lateral line area. However, there are no hard and fast rules about this, and in some mirror carp the scaling is further restricted to only the top of the back apart from small groups near the gill covers and tail root. Such carp are nearly, but not quite, leather carp. There are also fully-scaled mirror carp.

Distribution: Lakes, ponds, pits, reservoirs, slow rivers and the backwaters of fast rivers. Stocked in many waters all over England, less common in Wales, Scotland and Ireland. Irish carp are resident in Reynella Lake, Co. Westmeath, and Cork Lough.

Growth: 'Wildies' are relatively small common carp. A 10 lb (4·5 kg) fish is an exceptional catch. King carp are not considered notable until they reach 15 lb (6·8 kg). Specimen weight is 20 lb (9 kg) for domestic strains. Carp as large as 44 lb (20 kg) have been caught in England—from a water where fish at least 10 lb (4·5 kg) heavier have been observed at close quarters.

The Common Bream

Family CYPRINIDAE *Abramis brama*

Identification: The bream is an instantly recognizable fish. Its body is deeply oval, humped, and compressed from side to side. The mouth is large and thick-lipped. Baby bream (anglers call them 'skimmers') are silvery fish. Fully mature bream are darker: black-backed with subdued silver-tinged bronze flanks and dull grey fins.

Distribution: Lakes, pits, reservoirs, canals and rivers. Widely distributed in Ireland, most parts of England and in many lochs of the Scottish lowlands.

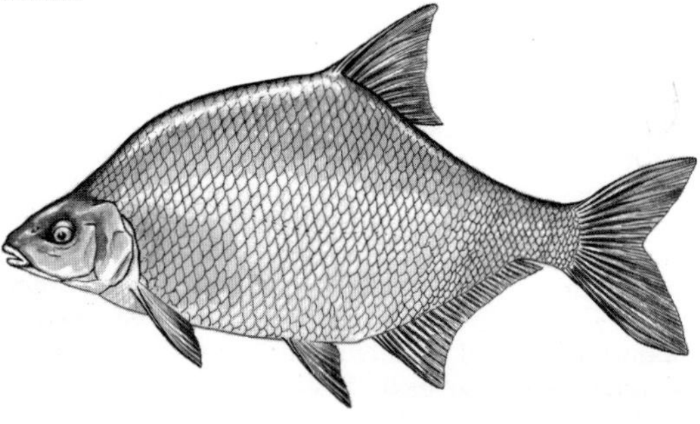

Growth: Big-growing, able to reach weights well above 10 lb (4·5 kg). Bream between 1 (450 g) and 6 lb (2·7 kg) are common catches, above 8 lb (3·6 kg) notable, and at 10 lb (4·5 kg) specimen size.

The Silver Bream

Family CYPRINIDAE *Blicca bjoerkna*

Identification: A silver bream is difficult to distinguish from a young common bream. The shape of both species is basically the same and, as its name suggests, the silver bream is silver-flanked—little different from a 'skimmer'. Absolute identification must be left to experts, but an outward difference is found in ray counts of the dorsal and anal fins.

	Common Bream	**Silver Bream**
Dorsal		
Unbranched	3	3
Branched	9	8
Anal		
Unbranched	3	3
Branched	23–28	19–23

Distribution: Restricted to eastern parts of England. Very rare elsewhere.

Growth: Silver bream larger than 3 lb (1·3 kg) have been recorded, but the general run of fish weigh less than 1 lb (450 g). A 'silver' of 1½ lb (680 g) is considered a splendid catch.

The Chub

Family CYPRINIDAE *Leuciscus cephalus*

Identification: A long sturdy-built fish. It has a big mouth set in a wide head and large scales. The back is olive green, the flanks dusky bronze and the belly white. All fins are dark with the exception of the coral red pelvic and anal fins.

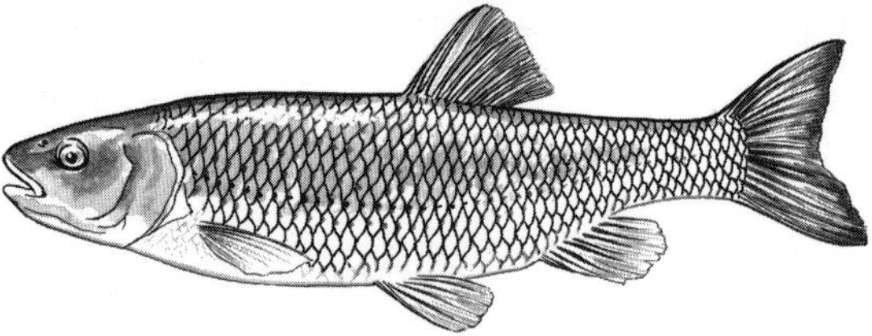

The following points avoid the confusion which frequently arises between small chub and big dace. The chub has a very big mouth compared with that of the dace, and a thicker, more blunt-headed appearance. The shaping of the fins is quite

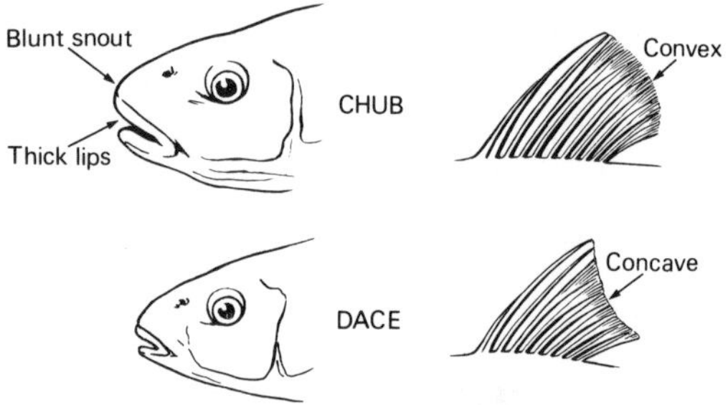

Points of identification between chub and dace

different too. The trailing edge of the chub dorsal is convex, that of the dace is concave. This difference also exists between the anal fins of the two species.

Distribution: Rivers and streams. Also found in a few lakes. Common throughout England apart from Devon and Cornwall. Less widespread (but very large-growing) in southern parts of Scotland. Rare in Wales and Ireland.
Growth: Average chub weigh between 1 (450 g) and 4 lb (1·8 kg). Five pounds (2·2 kg) is specimen weight for top-class chub rivers. It is probable that the species reaches 10 lb (4·5 kg) or more in British waters.

The Tench

Family CYPRINIDAE *Tinca tinca*
Identification: One of the most beautiful of our freshwater fishes. A stout fish, short for its depth. It has thick, smoky blue fins (the caudal fin spatular), small crimson eyes, and a silk-smooth body of rich golden yellow picked out with tiny close-packed scales. A rare ornamental variety, sometimes found in the wild, is the golden tench: bright orange or yellow all over, blotched with spots and patches of jet black.
Distribution: Lakes, ponds, canals, reservoirs, pits, slow rivers and the slacker sections of fast rivers. Well distributed in England, less so in Ireland—but heavy-growing in waters where it does occur, such

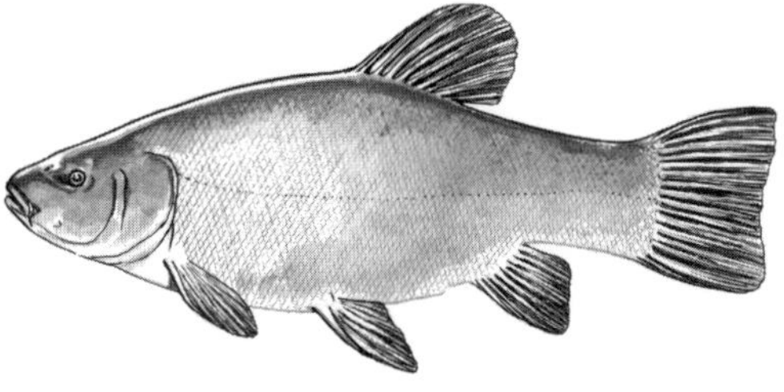

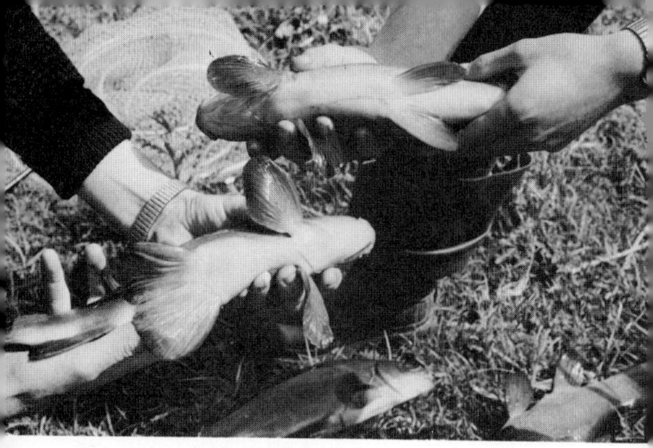

Male and female tench can be told apart by the shape of their pelvic fins. The pelvic fins on the male tench in the foreground are large and almost joined together. Those on the female are small and distinctly separate

as the River Shannon—and absent from Scotland. *Growth:* Most tench caught by anglers range in size from 1 (450 g) to 5 lb (2·2 kg). A 5 lb (2·2 kg) tench is specimen weight. Tench above 6 lb (2·7 kg) are very difficult to catch. The species grows at least as heavy as 10 lb (4·5 kg) under perfect conditions.

The Grayling

Family THYMALLIDAE *Thymallus thymallus*

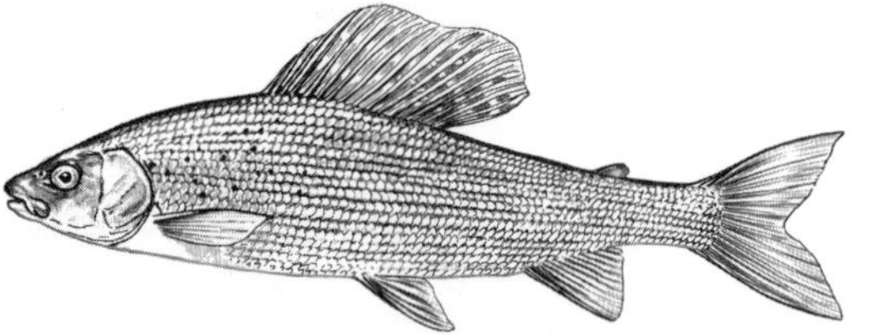

Identification: The grayling is a long streamlined fish, immediately identified by a large and colourful sail-like dorsal fin. There is also, further down the back towards the tail, a small fleshy stub, the adipose fin, indicating that it is as much a game fish as a coarse fish. The grayling is silver grey, marked over with darker lines running the length of its body. Its eyes are violet, a colour also mixed with subtle plays of blue and green in the shadings of the body.
Distribution: Well oxygenated rivers and streams. Widely scattered distribution in England, Wales and Scotland. Also stocked in a few lakes.
Growth: A 1 lb (450 g) grayling is a satisfactory size from most rivers. At 2 lb (900 g) it is big enough to be rated specimen weight. And at 3 lb (1·3 kg) plus most definitely the catch of a lifetime.

The Perch

Family PERCIDAE *Perca fluviatilis*
Identification: The aggressive nature of the perch is evident in its form and colour. A hump-backed fish, rough-skinned, markedly bold in the shaping of its head and mouth. The back is bronze green, flanks lighter, over-marked by strongly pronounced vertical stripes, and the belly bright white—sharply

contrasting with coral red pelvic and anal fins. The base lobe of the caudal fin is also red. There are two dorsal fins, the leading one armed with pointed spines.

Distribution: Waters of every size and type. Common in England, Ireland, Wales and southern Scotland.

Growth: Perch are splendid fish at 2 lb (900 g) weight. A 3 lb (1·3 kg) perch is a specimen.

The Pike

Family Esocidae *Esox lucius*

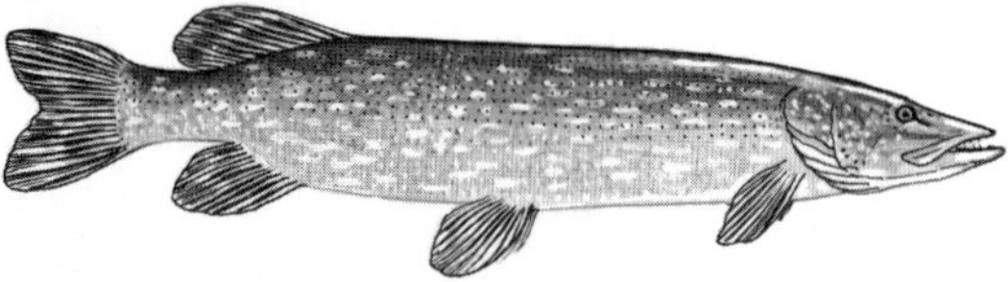

Identification: A lean ferocious fish is the pike—a confirmed predator both in appearance and in habit. It has vast, flattened jaws packed full with tiny, razor-sharp teeth, and a projectile-like arrangement of fins designed to facilitate the quick bursts of speed necessary to trap lesser creatures. Its greenish body, flecked heavily with pale yellow spots, is camouflage which blends perfectly with weeds, reeds and undercut banks where it lies to ambush its prey.

Distribution: Every type of water. Abundant throughout Britain and Ireland apart from north Scotland.

Growth: How big the biggest pike is is anybody's guess. Forty-pound (18 kg) pike have been taken on rod and line in the past. But huge as these fish seem, it is still not outlandish to suggest that in the lochs and loughs of Scotland and Ireland lurk pike approaching twice this weight. Twenty pounds (9 kg) is accepted specimen size. Any pike bettering 10 lb (4·5 kg) is reward enough for a day's effort.

The Zander or Pike-perch

Family PERCIDAE *Stizostedion lucioperca*

Identification: The zander, or pike-perch as it is also called, is not a hybrid between pike and perch but a distinctly separate species. It is a lean fish, large-mouthed and toothy, with a sharp-spined double-dorsal fin and transparent pectoral and anal fins. The back is dusk green, the flanks olive streaked with darker vertical stripes and blotches, and the belly white. Eyes are noticeably large.

Distribution: Lakes, slow rivers and canals. Localized in England, chiefly the Great Ouse Relief Channel and neighbouring waters such as River Delph, Great Ouse, Old Bedford River and the Middle Level Drain. Also Woburn Abbey lakes, and Claydon Park lakes (private). Presently increasing and spreading rapidly.

Growth: Capable of reaching weights around the 20 lb (9 kg) mark. A zander is a good fish at 8 lb (3·6 kg) and a specimen at 10 lb (4·5 kg). Nearly all the fish of 10 lb (4·5 kg) or more so far caught have been taken from the Relief Channel.

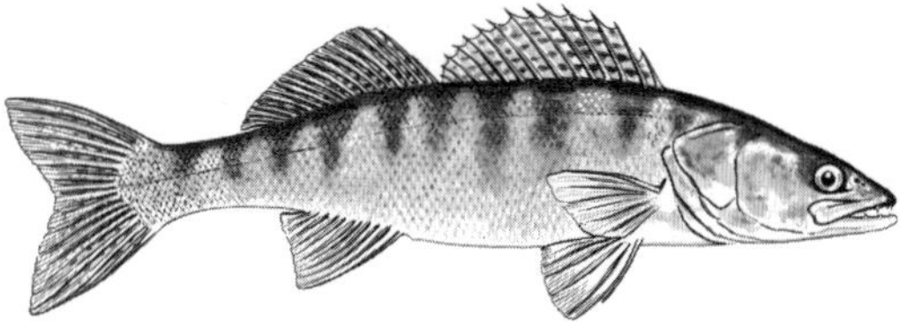

The Barbel

Family CYPRINIDAE *Barbus barbus*

Identification: A species indigenous to fast rivers. The back of the fish rises quickly from the nose to the shoulders, then sweeps down in a smooth line to the tail. The underside is flat, slightly concave. It is this shape of body which enables the barbel to hold position on the bottom in swift currents—the flow forcing against the lift of the back serving to press the fish downwards in the water.

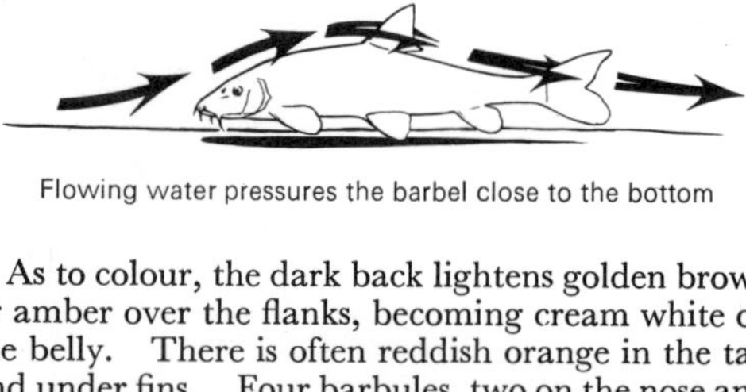

Flowing water pressures the barbel close to the bottom

As to colour, the dark back lightens golden brown or amber over the flanks, becoming cream white on the belly. There is often reddish orange in the tail and under fins. Four barbules, two on the nose and two at the join of the lips, hang down over a thick, underslung mouth.

Distribution: Fast rivers. A few lakes and reservoirs also contain barbel. In England the species is resident as far north as Yorkshire and as far south as Hampshire. It is not distributed further west than the Dorset Stour. Noted barbel rivers include: Dorset Stour, Hampshire Avon, Swale, Ure, Wharfe, Thames, Kennet, Lea, Bristol Avon and Severn. Stocking programmes have increased the distribution of the barbel considerably in recent years. The species is absent from Ireland, Scotland and Wales.

Growth: In top-class rivers a 10 lb (4·5 kg) barbel is a specimen. Elsewhere a 7 (3·1) or 8 lb (3·6 kg) fish is considered such. The barbel grows as large as 20 lb (9 kg) in the middle reaches of the Hampshire Avon.

The Eel

Family ANGUILLIDAE *Anguilla anguilla*

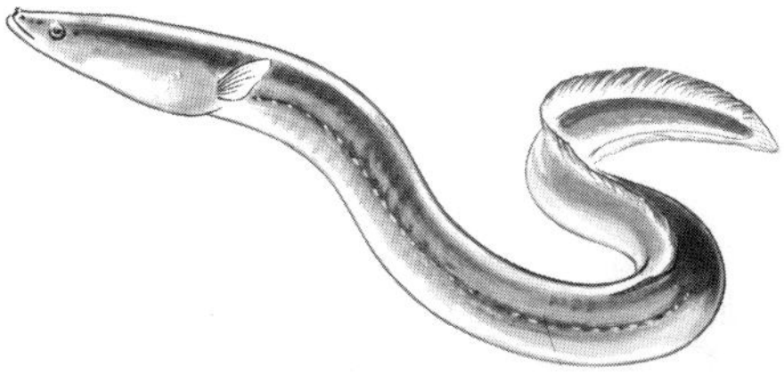

Identification: A snake-like fish unlikely to be mistaken for anything else. Usually dark grey above and yellow beneath, becoming more silvery overall during the autumn migratory period. Apart from the small pectoral fins, the remainder of the fins have evolved to form a continuous fringe extending two-thirds along the back, round the tail-end, and almost for the same distance up the underside.

Distribution: Widespread throughout Britain in every type of water.

Growth: In less enlightened times many fanciful theories were produced to account for the presence of eels. They had never been seen to breed and none of their eggs had ever been found, so consequently the ideas put forward were wildly imaginative.

Aristotle suggested that they developed spontaneously from mud. Pliny stated that hairs from horses' tails were their origin. Yet another belief declared that dew falling in late spring, after being heated by the sun, brought forth eels!

Today, though we still have much to learn about the life-cycle of the eel, we do at least know the location of the breeding-ground and the route the eels take to reach this country. It is a fascinating sequence of events.

Both European and American eels breed in an area of the Sargasso Sea situated roughly halfway between the Leeward Islands and Bermuda. From this cradle the minute European larvae set course in the North Atlantic Drift bound for our shores. As they journey so they change in shape and colour eventually becoming elvers—4 in (10 cm) long wrigglers, black and worm-like.

The elvers swim up coastal rivers after a journey which has taken three years to complete during April and May, gradually spreading into waters of all types everywhere. The years pass, and the elvers mature to adulthood and continue growing until the urge to spawn sends them swarming back to the rivers and down to the sea in search of the Sargasso breeding-grounds. This migration commences in autumn, but whether or not they actually reach their ancestral home is a moot point. Some authorities believe they do; others tend to think they perish on the way and that it is only eels returning from America which manage to return and breed successfully—thereby making possible future eel stocks for British waters.

Most eels caught by anglers are small ones, called 'bootlaces'. Apart from eating purposes they are of little interest to anglers. As regards large eels, a three or four-pounder (1·3–1·8 kg) is a nice one; at 5 lb (2·2 kg) or over, specimen size. It is not known to what weight eels grow in Britain. Twenty pounds (9 kg) would not be an unrealistic estimate.

The Wels or Catfish

Family SILURIDAE *Silurus glanis*

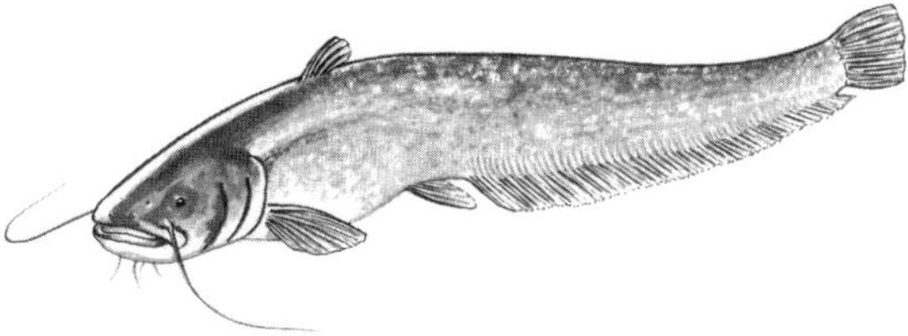

Identification: The wels, or catfish, could not by any stretch of the imagination be described as pleasant to look at. It has a big, flat, ugly head, and an extremely long, tapering, scaleless body. The mouth is massive, the lower jaw jutting out beyond the upper jaw, and there are six barbules: two long ones on the nose and four tiny whiskery ones beneath the chin. Of the fins, the dorsal fin is exceptionally small and the anal fin exceptionally long, fringe-like, extending half the length of the fish. A mixture of greys, greens and browns, mottled with irregular spotting, colours the upper parts. The lower parts are white.

Distribution: Strictly limited to a handful of still-waters in England. Claydon Park lakes (private)

and Woburn Abbey lakes are famous catfish preserves.
Growth: One of the largest species in the British Isles. In eastern Europe specimens have been recorded weighing 600 lb (272 kg). It is unlikely that catfish even one-sixth of that weight exist in England at the present time, but nevertheless, an 80 lb (36 kg) 'cat' is a possibility.

Legal Angle

Before setting out to catch coarse fish it is necessary first to obtain the legal right to do so. This right must usually be gained in two ways. (1) A rod licence, allowing the holder to participate in the sport of coarse angling. (2) A permit to fish a particular water from whoever controls the fishing rights.

Waters in England are administered by nine Regional Water Authorities, and in Wales by the Welsh National Water Development Authority. It is the R.W.A.s who issue, through tackle dealers, post offices, hotels and other agents, rod licences, valid for the length of one year, or a lesser period. An R.W.A. rod licence entitles the bearer to engage in coarse fishing, *using one rod*, anywhere within the issuing authority's area—providing permission of the person or body controlling the fishing rights is received first. If a second rod is required (a two-rod set-up is an advantage in some kinds of fishing) a second rod licence must be purchased.

A few waters are known as 'free waters'. That is to say, stillwaters and river stretches which can be legally fished by anybody in possession of a rod licence. Rather more private waters can some-

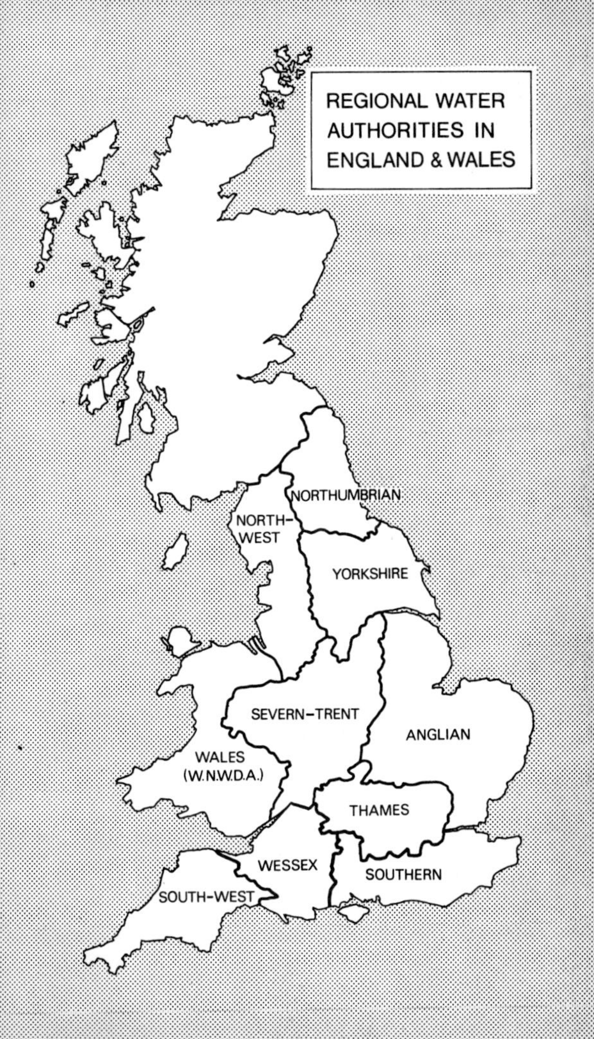
REGIONAL WATER AUTHORITIES IN ENGLAND & WALES
NORTHUMBRIAN
NORTH-WEST
YORKSHIRE
SEVERN-TRENT
ANGLIAN
WALES (W.N.W.D.A.)
THAMES
WESSEX
SOUTHERN
SOUTH-WEST

times be fished by applying to the owner and having that right granted at no cost. In such fortunate circumstances a rod licence is still of course required.

More usually, permission to fish must be paid for in the form of a day ticket, period ticket or season ticket, club membership subscription or syndicate share.

There are many ways of permit issue. By post, from a bailiff on the bank, from a tackle shop, from the home of the owner, or even from the local village store. Each water has a permit issue system which must be followed. Never start fishing without a permit assuming that 'somebody' will come along and collect the fee from you. Find out first if this is the system. If it isn't you may find yourself charged with an offence.

Now and then a water may be visited which does not require a rod licence. Here purchase of a permit automatically grants coverage, usually under a special rod licence—called a block or general licence—purchased by the owner or leaseholder from his R.W.A.

All this may sound a trifle complicated but in practice it is nothing of the sort. A visit to the local tackle shop and/or a letter to the secretary of the local angling club, will provide all the information required about licences and permits to fish waters available in your area. For waters further afield one can do no better than obtain a copy of *Where To Fish* (Harmsworth Press) or *Fishing Waters* (Link House Group). These invaluable publications, up-dated regularly, are packed with information which is useful to anglers on holiday and those who frequently travel to distant fisheries in search of sport.

In England and Wales the coarse fishing season extends from the 16th June to the 14th March inclusive. Outside this period, with few exceptions, it is illegal to deliberately angle for coarse fish. Nevertheless, the legal period *can* vary for different areas and individual waters, and this being so I suggest you always check this point for yourself to make absolutely sure.

In Yorkshire, for example, the season starts and finishes earlier by over two weeks (1st June to the 27th February inclusive). Moreover, along rivers where both coarse and game fishing is practised (e.g. the Hampshire Avon) certain stretches remain closed until well into summer, and may also close earlier too, to cater for the needs of salmon and sea trout enthusiasts.

The important thing about all this, is never to fish anywhere without the correct rod licence and permit, or indeed out of season. To do so is to invite trouble and almost certainly, in these days of tighter restrictions, the possibility of a court summons. The modern view of poachers is not anything like as friendly as once it was!

Rod licences and fishing permits include rules and regulations printed on their backs. Always read these sections carefully because the information contained varies from area to area. What is perfectly correct for one water may be absolutely banned somewhere else.

In Scotland and the Republic of Ireland, there is no close season or rod licence for coarse fishing. Most places can be fished without any payment, after obtaining permission from the owner. There is also no close season in Northern Ireland, but local regulations concerning rod licences and permits must be checked.

As well as observing the regulations indicated on licences, permits, and in club rule books, bankside notices must also be obeyed—likewise the accepted code of behaviour in the countryside. Such points as shutting farm gates, not lighting open fires, not throwing away unstubbed cigarette ends, parking the car where it will not obstruct, and leaving trees, shrubs, field crops, flowers and every kind of animal, as undisturbed as possible, are essentials of conduct which should be second nature to every angler.

Removal of litter is very important. Not only does litter not look attractive, it also kills and injures wild birds, small animals and expensive domestic stock. Reports of such incidents are common.

Taking home personal rubbish, and picking up rubbish left by less thoughtful individuals, is a joint responsibility in which we all have a part to play. Lengths of line, hooks, bottles, tins, plastic bags and cups, are objects we cannot afford to ignore. They are proven killers and a direct reason why certain waters are closed off completely to anglers.

Absolutely everything should be done to ensure that the countryside and its inhabitants, including fellow anglers, remains peaceful, happy and content.

Dress and Approach

Young fish, and stunted fish in over-populated waters, are invariably easy to catch. They are always hungry and not at all cautious. Beyond a general understanding of simple methods, very little skill is required to coax them to take hook-baits.

Larger, older fish, are a different proposition. They do not feed all the time, and when they do they tend to remain exceedingly shy of any unnatural disturbance which even slightly alerts in them a sense of danger. Fish of good size are more difficult to catch than little ones, and to stand any chance at all with them it is essential for the angler to remain as quiet and out of sight as possible.

In this respect a choice of clothing requires consideration. Whatever is worn—and anglers are very individualistic indeed about dress—it should be of sombre colour. Country greens and browns for preference. True enough, good fish are caught from time to time by anglers wearing white shirts and light-coloured trousers, but such captures are few and far between compared with the high total of fish which bolt for safety after becoming alarmed by unusual movements along the bank.

Fish do not see as we see, but they do see enough to recognize the abnormal. Greens and browns are the natural colours of the countryside, and clad in these colours the angler is far more able to blend with the scenery than would be possible wearing 'whiter than white' gear. Personally, I would no sooner go fishing in a white shirt than I would attend a wedding in hob-nail boots and overalls!

Keeping movement to a minimum is just as important. Don't walk about more than you have to. And when you do, keep well away from the bank-edge and off the skyline. Make use of available cover. Keep movements slow. Above all tread lightly. Fish are acutely sensitive to vibrations through the water, and when these emanate from land they quickly get the message and fade away to the cover of weeds.

A point to remember is that a combination of foliage and terrain is just as useful a hide when you are in front of it, as it is when you are behind it. Dressed in camouflaged gear, with a bush, tree trunk or high bank to your rear, you can still remain 'out of sight' from fish literally swimming at your feet in clear, shallow water. For example, perched

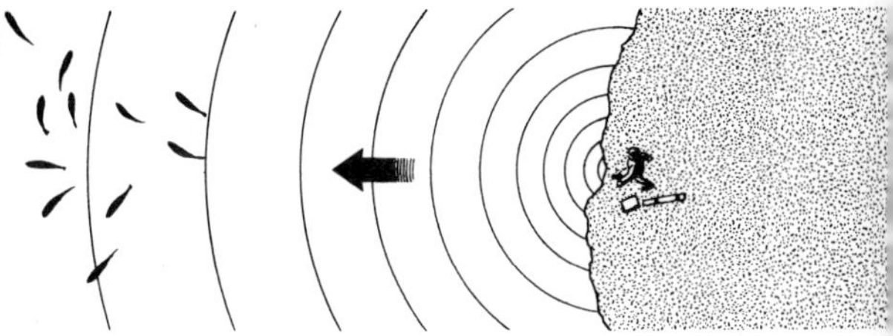

Heavy-footed movements scare fish

on the edge of a high bank an angler, and every movement he makes, is clearly outlined against the sky. But, by moving down in front of the bank he is able to make use of its face as an efficient means of back-camouflage, although much closer to the fish.

It is less likely that fish will be scared off when they are in deep or coloured water, or swimming far out from the bank, but the softly silent, unobtrusive approach, still remains sound tactics. The rule is never do anything which might even *possibly* put the quarry down, and that means the right clothes and the right approach on every fishing trip and in every situation. These are vital factors if you want to catch larger fish than run-of-the-mill tiddlers.

The bank face is useful back-camouflage

2: TACKLE, BAITS AND METHODS

Bait Fishing Tackle

Rods

The majority of rods are manufactured from hollow tapering tubes of fibreglass, a highly versatile long-lasting material which has virtually taken over from older rod-building materials such as cane and tubular steel. Rods in carbon-fibre (graphite) are also available, but these are very expensive compared with fibreglass equivalents and are not a recommended buy for complete beginners.

A 'glass' rod suitable for bait fishing has an overall length somewhere between 10 and 12 ft (3–3·6 m), a butt (handle) at least 2 ft (60 cm) long, and sliding fittings for attachment of the reel. The intermediate line guides, or rings, will be plain stainless steel ones finished with a hard chrome coating. Tip and butt rings will be lined with a friction-free material such as magnesium oxide.

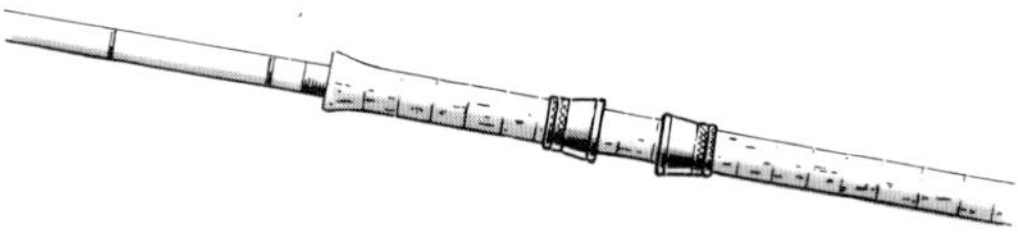

The rod butt (handle) is surfaced with cork

Rods have two or three sections which fit tightly together. The simplest tubular fibreglass join is known as 'wall-to-wall'—one section jammed inside another. Metal ferrule and modern spigot ferrule are more advanced types of join.

In putting a rod together check that the rings on the different sections all line-up exactly. If the rod has a metal ferrule the male part should be cleaned

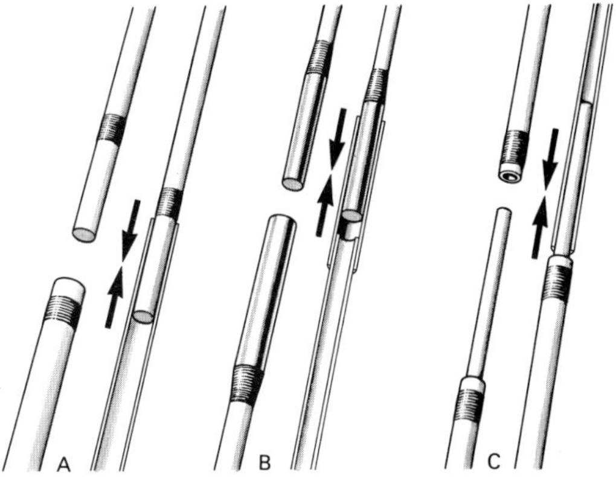

Ferrules: 'wall-to-wall' (A), metal (B), fibreglass spigot (C)

first and given a coat of spray-lubricant such as WD-40 or AP-75 to ensure that the sections will come easily apart again. A spigot ferrule requires a coating of graphite (from a pencil) to prevent it jamming. Do not force rod sections apart by twisting them in different directions. A *straight* pull is the correct drill.

To give you an idea of types of bait fishing rods, here are descriptions of favourite rods from my own collection.

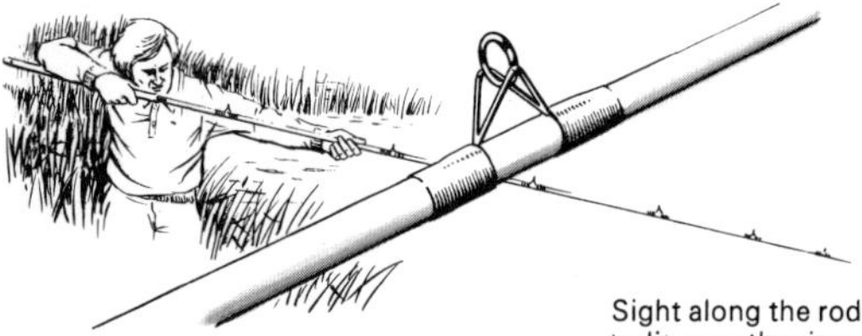

Sight along the rod
to line up the rings

Float Rod: Length 12 ft (3·6 m), weight 12 oz (340 g), action fast and tippy. Three-piece with wall-to-wall ferrules. A rod suitable for float fishing with lines less than 5 lb (2·2 kg) test.

Avon Rod: Length 11 ft (3·3 m), weight 8½ oz (240 g), action right through the rod. Two-piece with spigot ferrule. An ideal rod for freelining and legering as well as float fishing, matched with lines between 2 (900 g) and 8 lb (3·6 kg) test. This is an excellent design for the 'one rod' angler.

Big Fish Rod: Length 10 ft (3 m), weight 12 oz (340 g), through action. Two-piece with spigot ferrule.

Big Fish Rod: Length 11 ft 6 in (3·5 m), weight 1 lb (450 g), through action. Two-piece with metal ferrules and a detachable butt.

Big Fish Rods, with lines between 8 (3·6) and 15 lb (6·8 kg) test are for pike, carp, eel and zander. Also for hard-fighting smaller-growing species such as tench, barbel and chub in snaggy conditions and in waters where they grow to very large size.

Heavy Deadbaiting Rod (Beachcaster): Length 12 ft (3·6 m), weight 1 lb 12 oz (790 g), steep-taper action. Two-piece with metal ferrule. In coarse fishing the only use for this sea rod is to enable large weighty deadbaits (e.g. herring, mackerel) to be cast long distance when pike fishing from the bank.

The illustrations show the rods I have described.

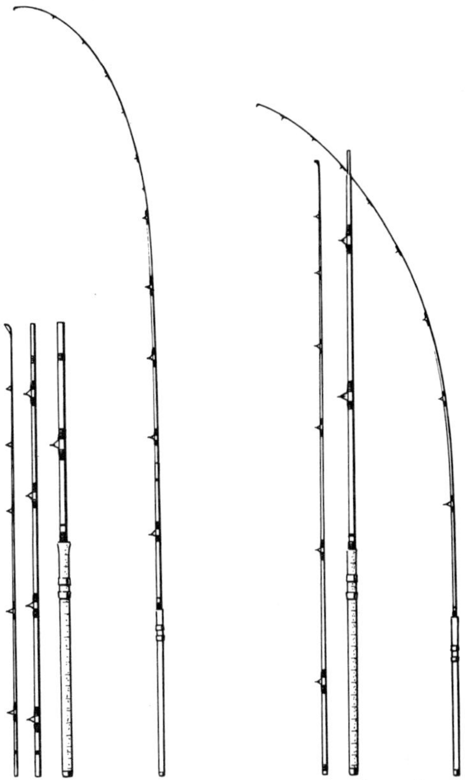

From left to right, tip-actioned float rod, through action Avon rod, through action big fish rod, steep-taper heavy deadbaiting rod.

The action of a rod is the shape of its curve when

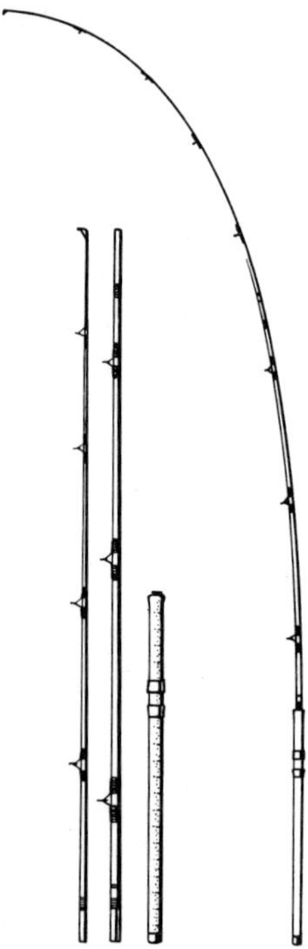

Big fish rod

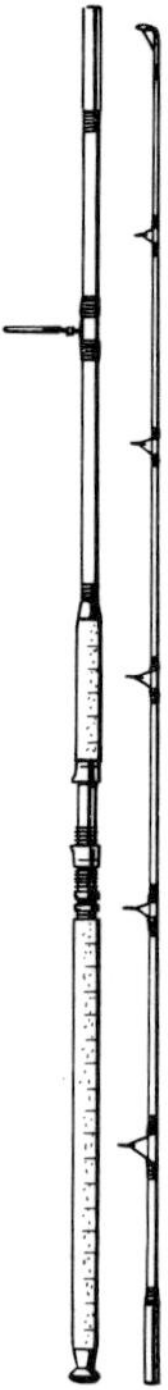

Deadbaiting rod

under pressure. Different actions are produced by varying the taper of the rod's length.

Rods are expensive and many newcomers to the sport will not be able to afford more than one to start with. Should this be the case, an Avon-type rod is the most sensible choice. This design is suitable for all small and middleweight species, pike in waters where they do not grow much over 10 lb (4·5 kg), and carp in open, snag-free lakes.

For big pike, eels, carp in weedy waters and middleweight species in similar conditions, a big fish rod is essential kit. Without such a rod these fish are better left well alone.

Fibreglass rods require little maintenance beyond drying them out at room temperature when they get wet, giving them a fresh coat of rod varnish as required, and checking the rings regularly for signs of grooving. Grooved rings damage the line, weakening its test strength considerably, and must be replaced without delay.

Shop-bought rods have a high-gloss varnish finish. They are nice enough to look at but a positive menace in sunny weather. The varnish reflects the sun, giving off 'flashes' which send fish dashing for cover each time a cast is made. This problem can be dealt with by giving rods a coat of matt-finish varnish to dull the gloss varnish down. Rods so treated do not look particularly attractive but they do increase the chance of catching fish—which is what rods are for after all!

Reels

The fixed-spool reel is by far the most popular type on the market at the present time. Many different designs are available, left- and right-hand wind, at a range of prices to suit the pocket of every angler.

A main feature of this reel is the adjustable slipping-clutch which, providing it is set correctly, will yield line to a hooked fish the instant it pulls extra hard or goes off on a powerful run. It is a device which helps prevent line breakage.

To set the clutch slipping, the tension nut on the front of the spool is eased with the line under a

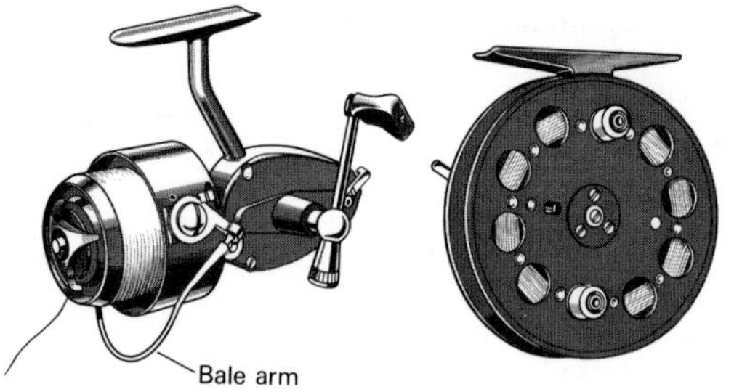

Fixed-spool reel (left) and centre-pin reel (right)

pressure approaching maximum test, until the spool just, and only just, begins to give line.

By placing the forefinger of the hand holding the rod against the rim of the spool a fine degree of control can be exercised over the slipping-clutch mechanism—lifting the finger when a fish pulls

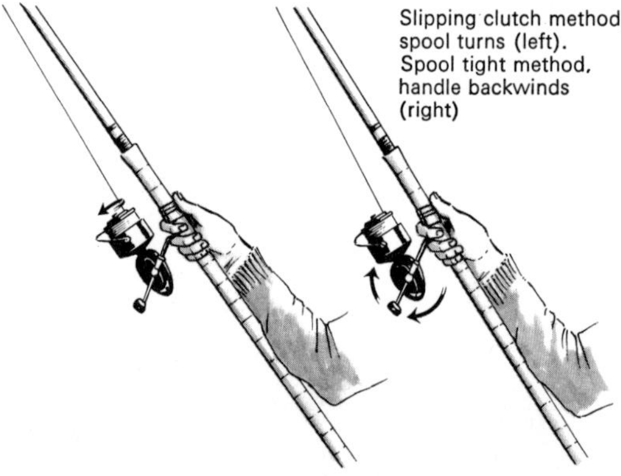

Slipping clutch method, spool turns (left). Spool tight method, handle backwinds (right)

hard and pressing it down firmly when pumping the rod up and down in order to wind line back on to the spool.

Alternatively, for anglers who do not like the slipping clutch routine (many don't) the spool can be screwed tight and the handle set to backwind against a running fish.

Line spools are interchangeable for fixed-spool reels and I suggest you buy several to allow a range of line strengths to be carried.

Fewer and fewer anglers use a centre-pin reel these days. The centre-pin design, although having some advantage over the fixed-spool with regard to tackle control when float fishing rivers is, in the final analysis, not nearly so versatile. It is also much more difficult to cast with efficiently.

By far the best plan for beginners is to learn the first principles of the sport with fixed-spool reels, and then later with two or three seasons' experience behind them, try a centre-pin as an alternative reel.

The side-cast reel is a cross between the fixed-

Side-cast reel, in casting position (left), and positioned for retrieving line (right)

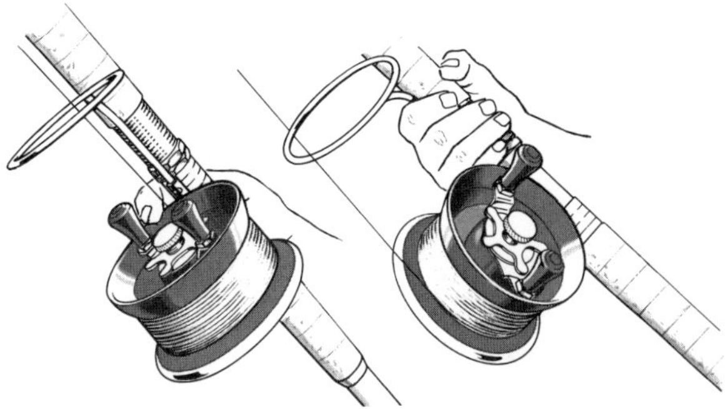

spool and the centre-pin. It is positioned as a centre-pin for retrieving line and playing fish, but for casting the drum twists round sideways so that the handles face up the rod and the line is able to slip freely over the edge in exactly the same way as from a fixed-spool. A large-diameter line-guide forms part of the fittings of this reel.

Side-casting unfortunately puts a multitude of turns in the line, and for this reason it is important to confine the use of side-cast reels to weightless tackle methods and terminal rigs which incorporate a large swivel at the top end for attachment to the main line. This swivel, plus winding the line firmly back on the drum through the fingers, virtually eliminates the turns completely.

Resting the butt against the forearm

For freeline deadbaiting in stillwaters I consider this type of reel second to none. The shallowness of the wide drum aids distance casting, and the centre-pin style of playing fish provides the sensitive control needed to handle big pike, eels and catfish.

All reels are mounted at the top of the butt so that the length of the butt rests comfortably against the underside of the forearm.

Lines

Nylon monofilament fishing line is available in a wide range of test strengths. If you have six spools for your reel this will enable you to carry the following breaking strains: 3 lb (1·3 kg), 5 lb (2·2 kg), 8 lb (3·6 kg), 12 lb (5·4 kg), and 15 lb (6·8 kg), with a spare spool available for any other test which might be required to suit a particular need. Each spool should be filled to the lip with at least 100 yd (91·4 m) of line.

To wind on a line, first fix the reel to the rod butt and attach the end of the line firmly to the spool. Then push a pencil through the hole in the container and get a friend to hold the pencil in such a way that the container revolves under pressure, as you transfer the line to the spool. Do this slowly keeping the turns tight. Care should be taken to spread the turns as evenly as possible as an aid to smooth casting, both for distance and accuracy.

Nylon monofilament has a nasty habit of losing strength quite suddenly, without warning, so test all lines regularly against a spring-balance. It may only be the last few yards (metres) of a line which has weakened, but check carefully because sometimes it is the whole line which needs replacing. It is sensible to commence each new season with fresh lines on all spools.

Fill the spool with line to the lip

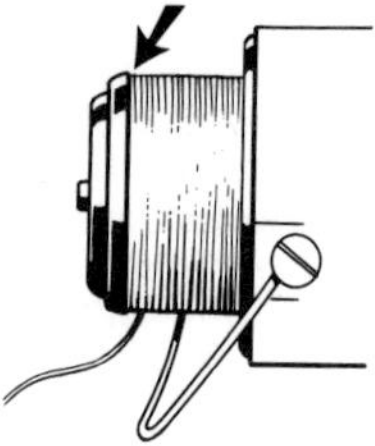

Winding on a line

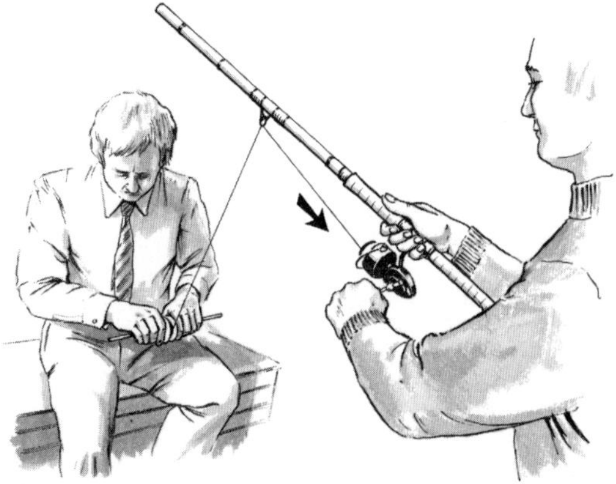

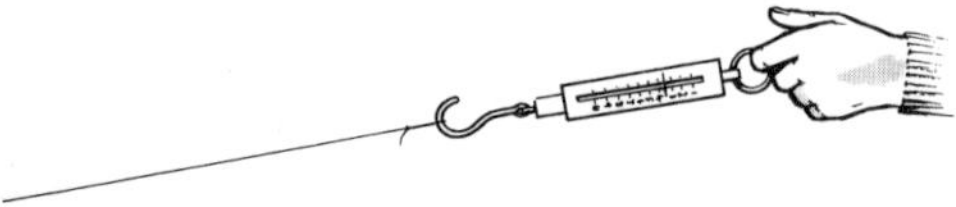

Check line strength against a spring-balance

Hooks

These can be bought attached to lengths of nylon, but personally I prefer loose hooks of the 'eyed' type which are cheaper and more reliable. Hooks ranging from size 2 (the largest) down to size 16 will be required—a quantity of each size in separate grip-edged plastic bags.

Small hooks are usually sharp enough as bought, but larger hooks will certainly require additional

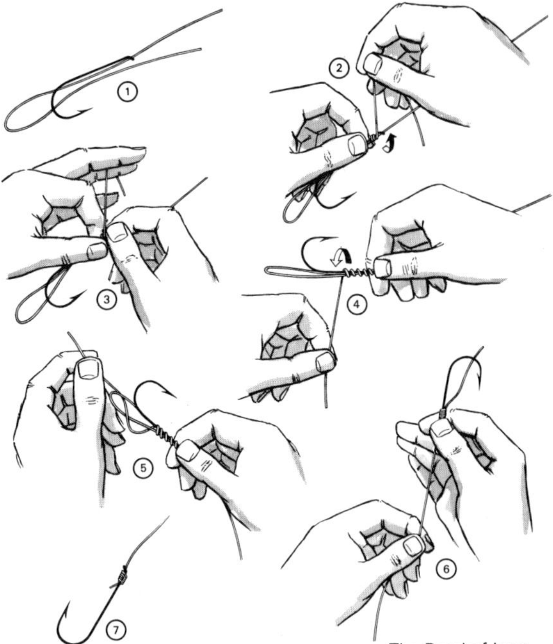

The Domhof knot

sharpening with a carborundum stone. Throw out any hooks which are spotted with rust, soft in the wire, or otherwise suspect. It is far better to be safe than sorry! Eyed hooks are attached direct to the reel line for maximum reliability. The Domhof knot is suitable for hooks with turned down eyes and the half-blood knot for hooks with straight eyes.

The illustration shows how the Domhof knot is tied. The end of the line is threaded through the eye and a loop formed along the length of the hook's shank (1). Several turns are then taken round the top of the shank with the right hand whilst the left hand retains the loop in place (2). Now the finger and thumb of the right hand are used to hold the turns firmly so that the left hand can be freed (3). Between three and five more turns are then made down the shank—making sure they do not overlap each other (4). The end of the line is tucked through the loop (5). The end of the line is pulled to remove the loop and tighten the turns (6). Neat and strong, the completed Domhof knot (7).

For pike and zander fishing a selection of three-point hooks will be needed for making up the wire traces for live and dead baiting methods. These treble hooks are numbered according to size exactly the same way as single hooks are.

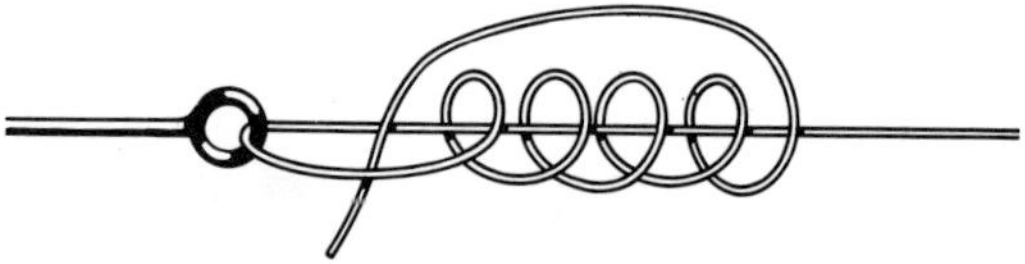

The half-blood knot for straight eyed hooks

Turned down eyed hook (left). Treble hook (right)

Trace Wire

When baiting with live or dead fish, or when lure fishing, for sharp-toothed predators such as pike and zander, some form of wire trace will be required between the main line and the hooks. Trace wire is either single-strand or multi-strand—the latter type also available nylon-coated. Single-strand wire is reliable for deadbaiting but, in my experience, is not so suitable for livebaiting or lure fishing because of its tendency to kink. A livebait as it swims about can cause kinking and so can a large, lightweight spoon which may double-back on itself. For lures and livebaits I prefer multi-strand wire which is soft and supple: plain for lures and nylon-coated for livebaits. I also use nylon-coated wire for most of my deadbait rigs.

On pages 91–97 will be found details of simple wire rigs and how to make them.

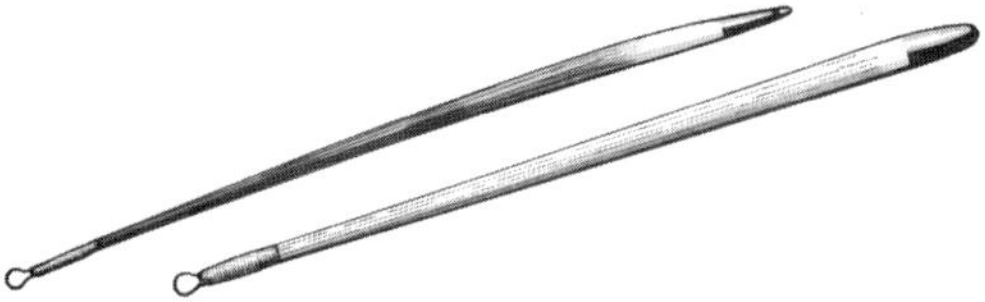

Simple floats from porcupine quill and balsawood

Floats

The purpose of a float is to indicate bites, to present the bait as naturally as possible at the depth the fish are feeding and, as required, to carry additional casting weight.

Float patterns are many and I appreciate that the vast array available in a tackle shop (including wagglers, duckers, sticks, zoomers, windbeaters and darts, etc.) can bewilder the tyro. Enough to say at this point that it is not necessary to own hundreds of floats to catch fish. A handful of different patterns will suffice to begin with, and these will be mentioned in the parts of this book dealing with basic methods and practical fishing. (See pages 102 and 130.)

Floats are made from such materials as bird quills, porcupine quills, cane, balsawood, cork, wire, reed, elderpith and nylon, or often a combination of two or three of these materials.

To attach a float to the line a small ring is whipped to the lower end and a rubber band (float cap) is added near the tip. For some methods this ring is most useful, but for straightforward attachment there is nothing to beat two strong rubber bands—one near the tip and one near the base.

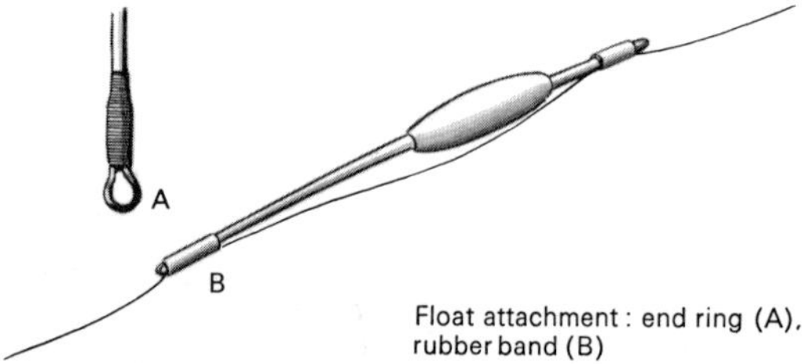

Float attachment: end ring (A), rubber band (B)

This allows quick interchange of floats to be made without the need to take down the terminal tackle.

Float caps are bought in packets of assorted sizes. Be a bit choosy about the brand. Float caps must be long enough and strong enough to grip the float against the line firmly and prevent it sliding down during casting and retrieving. Depth setting must be kept exactly right to catch fish with a float rig, and weak float caps can spoil the techniques very easily.

Lead

To 'cock' a float, make it stand in the water with just the right amount of tip showing above the surface; lead split-shot is added to the line beneath the float. The line is placed in the split and the split closed with either finger pressure or thin-nosed pliers—but not too tight because this can damage the line and even cut it through.

Split-shot is available in different sizes. The largest is called swanshot. Other sizes include AAA, BB, and microshot. There are also types of shot which are numbered according to their size. An easy way to obtain a supply of shot is to buy a multi-compartment dispenser containing six different shot sizes.

For float fishing use only soft-lead shot. If you cannot close the split with average finger pressure, it is not soft enough. Most shot is round, but another type, a very splendid type for float work, is called 'mouse droppings'—elongated shot made from super-soft lead.

Apart from its use for float fishing, lead-shot is also used when legering to make a simple form of leger weight known as the link-leger. There are a number of variations on the same principle, but I make my link-legers as follows. A 2 in (5 cm) length of monofilament, test strength slightly less than the main line, is attached to a tiny two-way swivel, and to this 'tail' is added swanshot made from hard lead. By varying the amount of shot it is possible to balance the weight of the link-leger exactly right for the swim being fished, adding or subtracting shot as required.

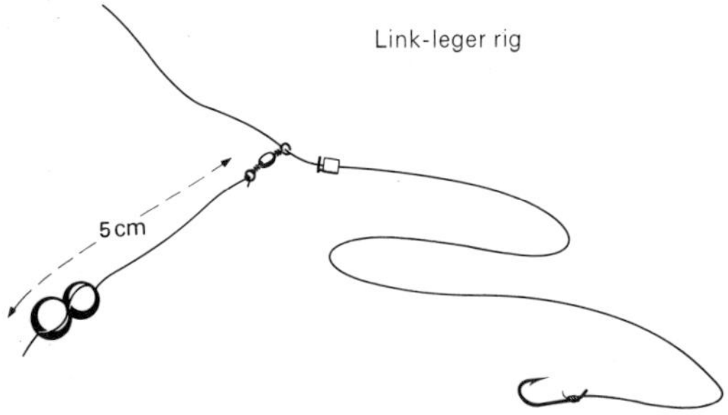

I use the link-leger for both stillwater and river fishing. I consider it an outstanding general-purpose weight. To attach it to the line, the line is threaded through the top eye of the swivel, a plug-stop is added, and finally the hook is tied on.

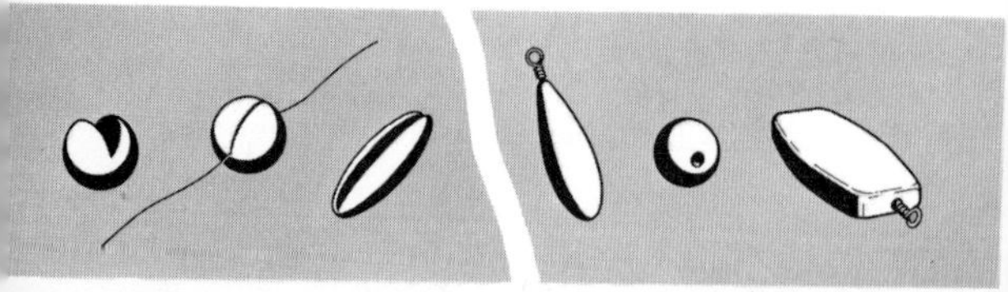

Split-shot, and, from left to right, three leger weights: Arlesey bomb, drilled bullet, swivelled coffin lead

Other leads to have in the tackle box include Arlesey bombs and swivelled coffin leads. Carry a few of each in ¼ oz (7 g), ½ oz (14 g), and ¾ oz (21 g), sizes. For piking, ½ oz (14 g), 1 oz (28 g), and 2 oz (56 g) drilled bullets are handy leads.

New leads are shiny. They dull quickly in the water, but if you want to avoid every chance of scaring fish, leave them in a jar of vinegar overnight. That will do the trick.

As bought, a coffin lead is not swivelled. Insert a two-way swivel for half its length inside one end of the lead and bang it firm with a hammer.

Plastic plug-stops

To hold the leger weight up the line at a set distance from the hook some form of stop is needed. One or two split-shots is a commonly used method, but a better device is the plastic plug-stop. This consists of a stiff plastic band fitted with a specially shaped plug. The line is threaded through the band and the plug jammed in to hold it tight.

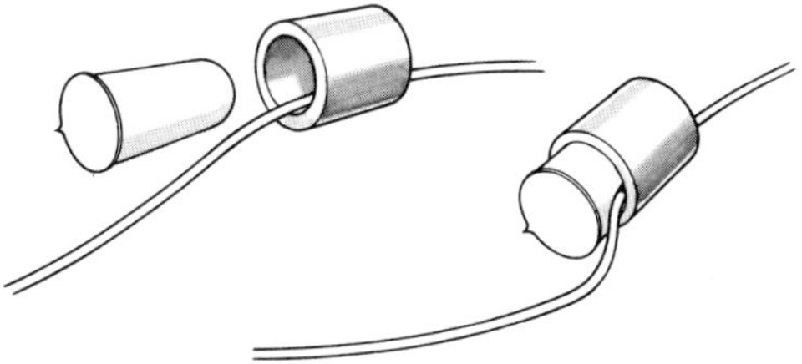

Plastic plug-stop

Swimfeeders

These are fished in place of the leger lead—with the additional advantage that they feed the swim with groundbait and hookbait samples.

The basic swimfeeder is a transparent plastic tube perforated with holes and weighted by means of a lead strip. There is a loop of nylon at one end and to this loop a link-swivel is added. The main line is threaded through the eye of the swivel.

In operation one end of the tube is plugged with groundbait, a 'middle' of hook bait samples is added, and then a cap of groundbait to seal it. Cast out, the groundbait breaks-up and the contents are spilled out on the bottom right where the hook-bait is lying.

The open-end swimfeeder is best for stillwaters. The type more suitable for rivers is known as a block-end swimfeeder, designed to let the feed out in a slow trickle rather than all at once.

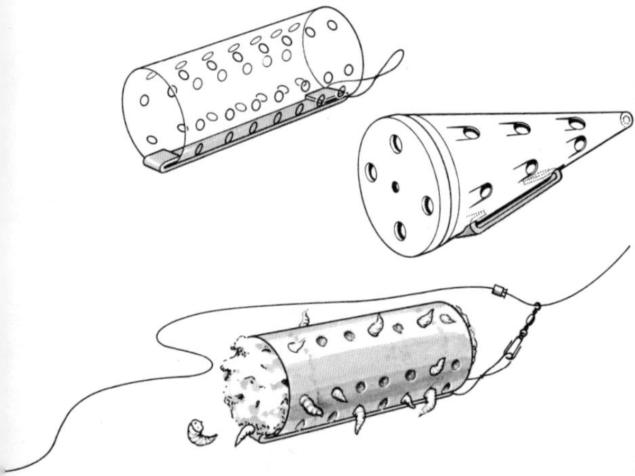

Top : open-end swimfeeder. Centre : Polycone block-end swimfeeder. Bottom : open-end swimfeeder primed with bait

An advanced block-end design is known as the Polycone. This type is attached by threading the line through a central hole and retaining it above the hook, running leger style, by means of a plug-stop or split-shot. The Polycone discharges its contents at a slower rate than the open-end, and it has a shape which is less likely to roll along the bottom or to lift in swift water—features very important in a swimfeeder used for river fishing.

Another excellent block-end feeder is the Feeder-link. Designed by Peter Drennan, this is one of the very best for legering in rivers.

Rod Rests

Some fishing methods require the rod to be rested steady, either because the technique is delicately sensitive or because there will possibly be long waits between bites—bites from species which hang on

Rod rests

long enough to allow the angler time to pick up the rod and strike. Rod rests are used for this purpose.

A rod rest for front support has a groove beneath the fork so that the line can run freely out. The back rest is a plain half-moon shape. Telescopic rests (front and back) allow for fine adjustment. They should have stout shafts and strong tips.

Front and back rests are angled so as to bring the rod butt close alongside the angler. This arrangement enables the rod to be picked up and a bite struck all in one movement.

Landing Nets

Apart from the smallest tiddlers, a landing net will be required to lift fish from the water. A triangular-framed landing net with 32 in (81 cm) arms is a reasonable size for most species apart from the very

David Carl Forbes carefully unhooks a tench. The wet mesh of the landing net helps prevent damage to the protective slime coat of the fish

Landing nets

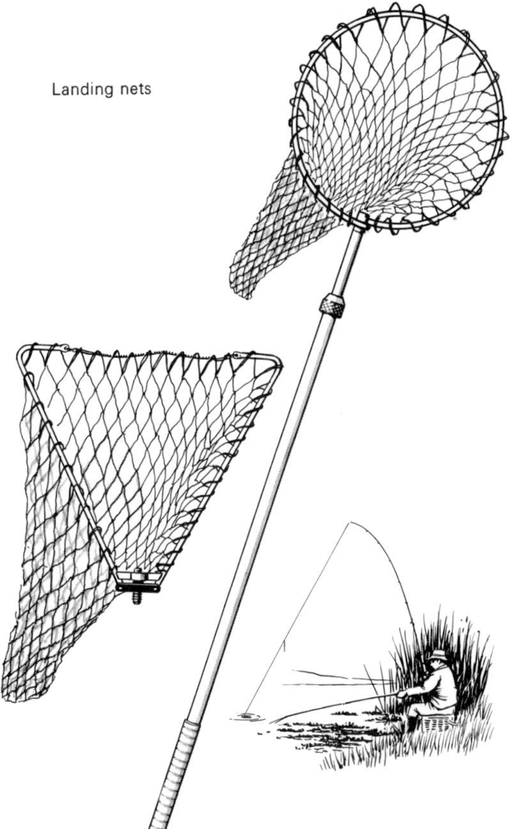

largest carp and pike, etc. For big fellows a landing net with 42 in (106 cm) arms is a more adequate size. Round-framed nets are also available and these are useful for netting fish from thick weed as they penetrate the growth more easily than triangular-framed nets.

The handle should be strongly built, featuring a reliable screw-fitting for joining to the frame. An extending handle is priceless when attempting to net a fish from across a wide margin of weed or soft marsh.

How to net fish correctly is explained in the chapter dealing with handling fish. (See pages 166–168.)

Polarising Glasses

A pair of these glasses is a marvellous angling aid. They absorb reflected glare so that only useful light reaches the eye. When the sun is strong on the water the surface loses its brilliant sheen and it becomes easier to see the float clearly and bite indications.

Polarising glasses also enable the angler to see right through the surface, deep into the water—as far as the bottom, providing the depth is not too great or the water too murky. In this way big fish can be pinpointed and fished for specifically. For maximum effect, wear a wide-brimmed hat or eye shield.

Plummets

The typical plummet is a cone-shaped lead weight with a ring at the pointed end and a thickness of cork let into the base. It is used to discover the depth of a swim when float fishing. The hook is threaded through the ring and secured in the cork. By casting out several times and adjusting the float either up or down until just the right length of tip pokes above the surface, the tackle can be set to

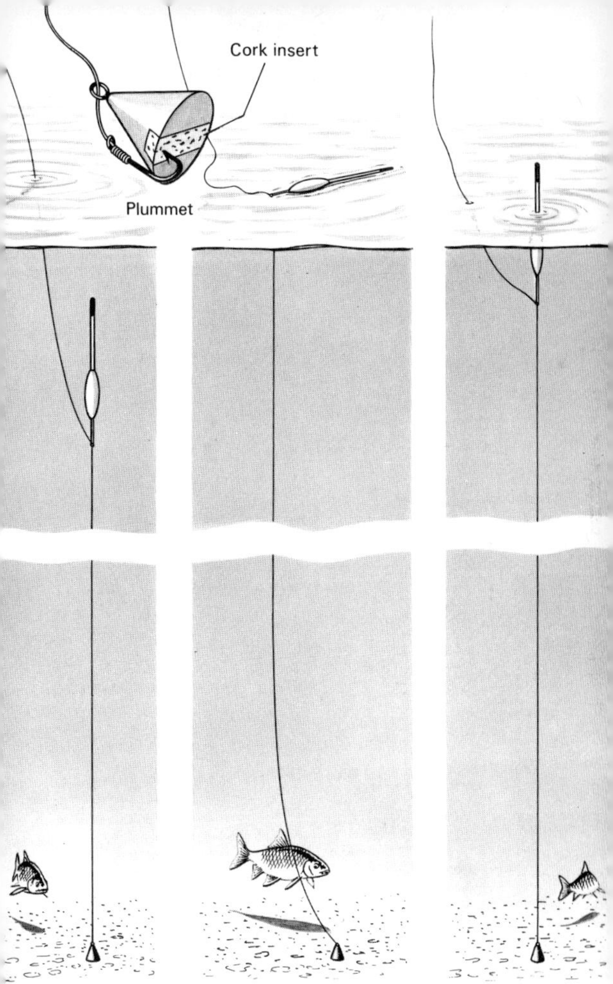

Left to right, the float is under depth, over depth and at correct depth

swim depth. A plummet is mainly useful for still-waters of great depth rather than shallow lakes and rivers.

Seats

Collapsible seats suitable for angling purposes come in many shapes and sizes. The main requirements of any seat is that it should be both strongly built

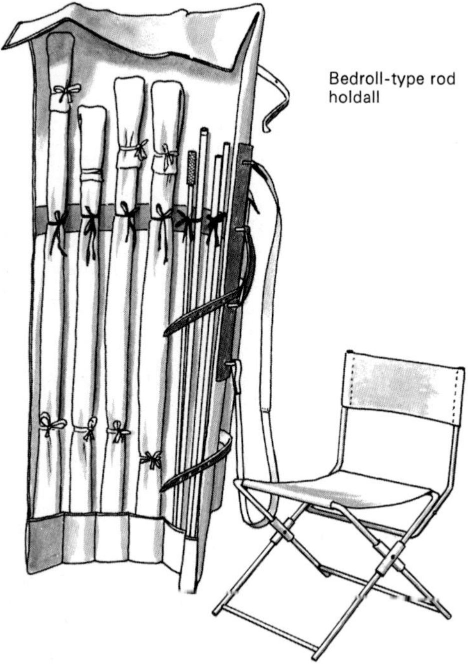

Bedroll-type rod holdall

and comfortable. Low seats, which allow advantage to be taken of minimum cover, are better for daytime fishing than high ones. At night, all types of seat, bedchairs included, can be used.

Choose a design which features a backrest for additional comfort. If it also has armrests, make sure it is wide enough to sit in without becoming so firmly stuck that when you stand up to play a fish the seat remains with you! This can happen if you are wearing thick clothing.

Rod Holdalls

Rods, rod rests, landing net and umbrella, can be carried in a holdall fitted with a shoulder strap. Three main patterns are available: one with zip-up top, one with a full length zip which opens up wallet-style, and one which opens right out like a bedroll. The choice is yours, but having tried them all I now prefer the latter, which gives easier access to everything. It features individual sections for rods, rod-rests, landing net and umbrella, all securely held and protected.

Arrangement of tackle

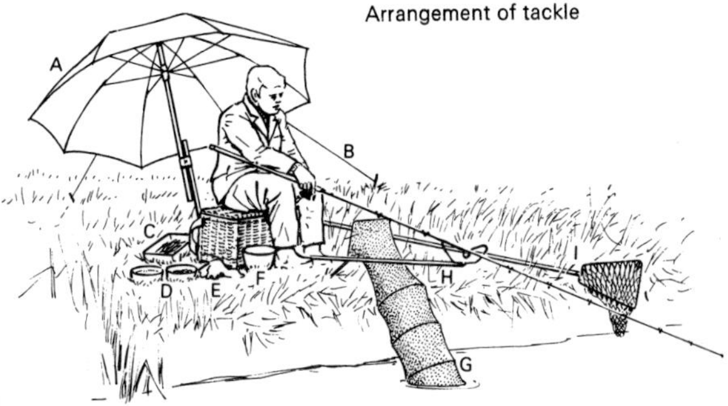

Tackle Carriers
Tackle boxes, baskets and haversacks are used to carry tackle, bait and refreshments. The choice is again one of personal opinion. Boxes and baskets have the advantage that they can also be used to sit on, but large haversacks hold far more gear.

Other Tackle
Scissors, knife, torch, thermometer, old towelling and a first-aid kit are essentials. An anti-sting spray such as Wasp-eze should be included in the first-aid kit.

A large umbrella, complete with metal pegs and guy ropes to stake it firmly down, and a waterproofed canvas sheet, are further accessories which make the coldest rain-filled day pleasantly bearable —even if the fish do decide not to bite!

Tackle should be arranged so that essential items are close to hand. The illustration shows a proper layout of gear. An umbrella (A) is both a shelter from the rain and a windbreak. It should always be staked down, to prevent it blowing away, with guy ropes and metal pegs (B). Floats, hooks and shot (C), hook baits (D), hand-towel (E) and groundbait (F) are all items which should be located within arm's reach. The mouth of the keepnet (G) is best positioned so that the fish can be slipped inside without the need to stand up. If a rod rest (H) is used it should be angled so that strikes can be made firmly over the shoulder. Never commence fishing without first fitting up a landing net (I) and placing it on the bank where it will be ready for instant action when needed.

Choosing Tackle
By far the most sensible plan is to visit a recommended tackle shop, in the company of a know-

ledgeable angling friend if possible, and let the dealer advise you in your selections according to what you can afford.

Tackle dealers are keen anglers themselves, and what is more they rely for their livelihood on clients who return regularly. They cannot afford to give bad advice or mislead, and their after-sales service and deep knowledge of local angling cannot be equalled by any form of mail-order tackle buying or by traders selling tackle purely as a sideline.

Casting

Short casts are made underhand. The terminal tackle hangs down rather less than the length of the rod, with the bale-arm open and the forefinger against the spool rim to prevent the line spilling free. As the rod top is moved down and outwards, a sharp flick is given to the tackle and at the same time the forefinger is lifted to release the line.

Longer casts are made across the body. The bale-arm is switched to the open position, and the

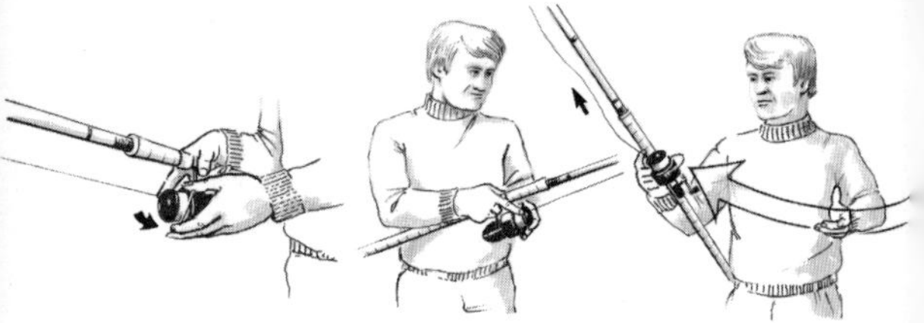

line retained by a forefinger. In a single movement the rod is brought across the body and, as the terminal rig straightens out astern of the angler, the rod is brought back again to point in the direction

of the cast. As that angle is reached the forefinger is lifted to free the line and send the terminal tackle on its way.

Alternatively the cast can be made away from the body.

Distance casting a deadbait with a beachcaster and side-cast reel combination is actioned as follows. First, the deadbait is set to hang down approximately half the length of the rod, and the reel drum turned to the casting position with the forefinger of the hand nearest to the reel pressing against the rim of the drum as a line stop.

Now the angler positions himself and his tackle (1). A pendulum action is imparted to the bait, first away from the body (2), and then back towards the body (3), *directly in line with the length of the rod.* On the second outward swing (4) the angler stretches well over ready to propel the bait forward by pulling down on the butt end with the left hand and pushing upwards from under the reel with the right hand (5). The angle of the body and the rod are shown (6) as the tackle is released.

Note the changing position of the head as the cast develops. This cast is made slowly, without jerk, and with maximum power applied from position 5 right through until the bait is released.

Hookbaits and Groundbaits

Bread

The most versatile of all baits. *Bread flake* is a piece torn from the inside of a fresh loaf pinched round the hook-shank to hang down soft and flaky over the hook. A pinch of flake combined with maggots forms a highly successful 'sandwich bait'.

Bread crust is a chunk torn or cut from the outside of a loaf so that a portion of the white remains attached. To use this bait the hook is inserted from the crust side, turned, and brought back through so that the bend of the hook rests against the inside part. Crust can be fished freeline at the surface, or anchored with a leger weight at any depth from bottom to surface.

Bread cube is a shape about the size of a sugar lump, with or without the outer skin attached. Notable as bait for big roach.

Bread paste is made by removing the crust from a three-day old loaf, wrapping the white inside a clean cloth and giving the contents a thorough soaking. As much water as possible is then squeezed out and the bread, still in the cloth, is worked with the fingers until it is a soft smooth paste.

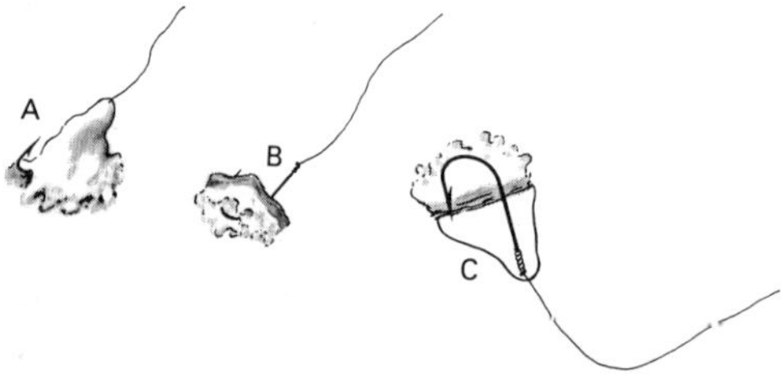

Bread flake (A), bread crust (B), balanced crust (C)

Balanced crust combines a buoyant crust with enough paste added to the hook-shank to sink it ultra-slowly.

Caddis larvae

These are the grubs of the caddis fly which live along the bottom of rivers and lakes in little tubes which they construct from twig fragments, leaf remains and grit. A caddis grub must be extricated carefully and nicked on the hook through the tip of the tail.

Cheese

Cheddar cheese, in cube or paste form, is a fine general-purpose bait. Chub, roach, barbel, carp and tench, have special liking for it. All other kinds of cheese can be used—the softer, strong-smelling ones, mixed with bread paste.

Crayfish

Supplies of these small freshwater lobsters are obtained after dark, from certain rivers, by the drop-net method. A suitable drop-net can be made from the wheel rim of a child's cycle by adding a narrow-mesh bottom, three or four steadying wires and a length of cord for lowering and retrieving the apparatus. A fish such as a herring is attached firmly in the middle of the net as lure, and the trap is then dropped to the bottom against the edge of the bank.

It is advantageous to have a number of nets out along a suitable stretch. Each net is left for at least 30 minutes and then retrieved quickly. With any luck several crayfish will have crawled over the netting to eat the bait-lure; they must be picked up between finger and thumb across the back before they have a chance of scuttling off into the vegetation.

A second way of catching crayfish is to wade a

Crayfish drop-net baited with a dead fish (arrowed)

small stream turning over the larger stones under which they rest during daylight hours. As the crayfish are exposed, pin them down with a forked stick to be lifted out with the fingers.

A crayfish bait is fished freeline on a size 4 hook passed through the tail-end segment from the underside. Lead is only added if the weight of the bait is not enough to hold position against the strength of the current. Crayfish can be kept alive in a large bucket of water, if the water is changed frequently.

Creepy-crawlies

This category includes such animals as beetles, woodlice, caterpillars, dockgrubs and snails.

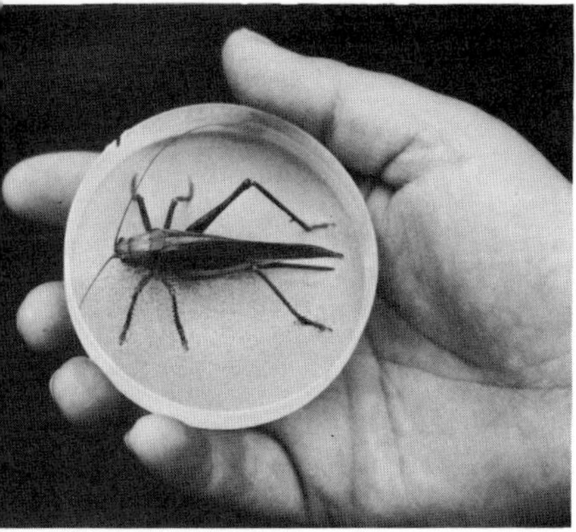

Giant grass-hoppers (when they can be found) are fine bait for chub

These, and similar small creatures, are well worth trying as bait.

Elderberries
Ripe for picking from late summer onwards. The berries can be used straight off the tree, nicked lightly on fine-wire hooks to avoid bursting, for roach, dace, chub and barbel. To preserve elderberries for out-of-season use put them in either syrup or a solution of one part formalin to ten parts water.

Elvers
These young eels, just a few inches long, can be collected from coastal rivers during spring. Preserve them in a formalin solution or keep them alive in an old bathtub. They can also be obtained throughout the summer months by searching weed clumps and underneath the bank with a collecting net. Elvers are fished on float and leger rigs. The live ones should be killed first by dipping them in boiling water. A freshly dead elver hooked through

the head and long-trotted down the length of a weirpool in June is first-class bait for chub—and barbel too, when the mood takes them.

Fish baits
Minnows, loach, ruffe, bullhead, bleak, gudgeon, roach, rudd, dace, carp, bream, chub, perch, herring, mackerel and sprat, are all baits for catching predators: pike, perch, zander, eels, chub and catfish.

Flies
Alive and dead, flies of various kinds can be used to catch surface-feeding fish. Freshly hatched bluebottles are outstandingly suitable and easy to obtain. All that is required is an airtight tin full of casters (chrysalid stage) left in a warm spot to hatch. If kept in the container the majority of the flies remain in a doped state, unwilling to fly. This makes possible their removal one at a time for the hook without risk of the whole lot swarming free.

Freshwater mussels
Found in both stillwaters and rivers they can be harvested with either a long-handled rake or a forked stick and glass-bottomed observation tube. Never remove more than you absolutely require, and return any left at the end of the day. Keep them alive in a keepnet. The shell is opened with a knife and the soft flesh threaded as firmly as possible on the hook. When removing the flesh keep an eye open for pearls. Freshwater mussel pearls of quality are worth a great deal of money. Mussel bait is deadly for tench and bream on the right day.

Hempseed
To prepare hempseed it should be soaked for a few hours, then boiled in water with soda added until

the husks split exposing the white kernels. Fine-wire hooks are used when single-seed float fishing for roach and dace, the bend of the hook being pressed into the white split to hold the seed in place. Hempseed is also legered for barbel and chub—two or three grains on a big hook.

More controversy surrounds the use of hemp as bait than all the other baits put together. A lot of nonsense has been preached about the seed drugging fish and making fisheries 'one-bait-only' waters, and consequently it is banned in some places. Check this point locally before using it.

When fishing with round split-shot and hempseed on the hook false bites are often registered caused by fish sucking the shots in mistake for seed. This irritation can be avoided by shotting the tackle only with mousedropping split-shot or coiled lead wire. Lead wire is attached by threading the line through the coil and holding it in place with a single dust-shot or plug-stop.

Wheat, pearl barley, corn on the cob, macaroni, tares and long-grain rice, are baits prepared in much the same way as hempseed.

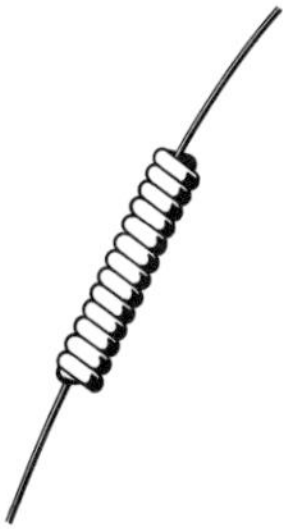

Lead wire coil for hempseed fishing

Tinned sweetcorn

This bait requires no preparation, simply impale one or more grains on a fine-wire hook. Sweetcorn attracts large fish of many species, and at the same time avoids the little ones.

Maggots

Without doubt the most popular bait. Maggots, or gentles, are the larvae stage of the bluebottle fly. All species apart from confirmed predators can be caught on them, including large specimens.

Maggots are fished single, double, or as a bunch of a dozen or more, legered and float fished. The smaller maggots of the house fly (squats) and the greenbottle fly (pinkies) have purpose as free-feed when hookbaiting with blue-bottle maggots.

Casters is the angler's name for chrysalids, the stage which maggots pass through prior to hatching as mature flies. They are yellow at first, becoming bright orange and then dark red prior to transformation. Casters are fished neat or in conjunction with maggots; two maggots and a single caster is a typical sandwich bait.

Some casters float and some sink. It is important when feeding a swim with them as groundbait that only sinkers are used. Floaters and sinkers can be divided by tipping them into a bucket of water and skimming off those which remain at the surface.

Floating casters are, however, bait for surface fishing methods. Scattered on the water they attract such fish as rudd and dace.

Meat baits

Sausages are excellent bait for barbel, carp and chub. I prefer the small skinless varieties, uncooked, lightly fried or lightly boiled, whole or cut into chunks. Sausage meat is equally good mixed with bread or sausage rusk to form a paste.

Cubes of tinned meats and liver are other proven meat baits. And so too are exotic 'stink baits' concocted from cat and dog foods mixed with rusk, bread, and anything else which is meaty smelling.

Potatoes

Mainly bait for carp, but also at times used for tench, bream and chub. Tinned potatoes are best for short-range freeline fishing, and larger unskinned potatoes for distance casting and for reducing the interest of other potato-loving species when angling solely to catch carp.

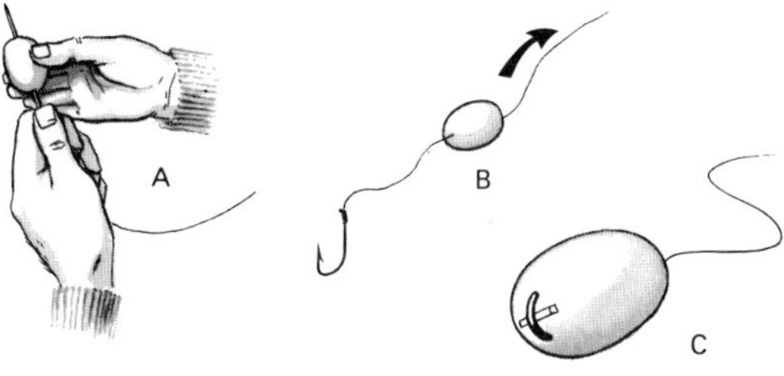

Baiting with potato bait

Potatoes are prepared by boiling them until they are soft, as soft as would be required for table. To bait a potato the line is threaded through with a baiting needle (A). The hook tied on and pulled back against the bait (B). For short-ranges the bait is tossed out by hand, but for rod casting a shock absorber is needed between the hook-bend and the bait. A piece of crust or half a matchstick is suitable for this purpose (C). Carp are caught on both skinned and unskinned potatoes. A thick disc-shape, because it sinks slowly, is ideal when fishing

Potato disc, for a muddy or weedy bottom

over thick mud or bottom weed. It is less likely to become hidden.

For species other than carp, cube portions of potato work well. In order to hand-cast a potato,

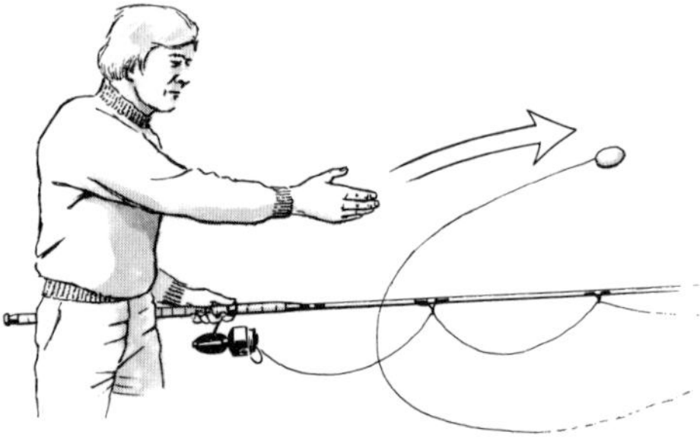

Hand-casting a potato

the bale-arm of the reel is disengaged so that line can run freely, and the rod is pointed in the same direction as the bait is to be thrown.

Silkweed

Silkweed, or rait, is a soft algae found growing on weirpool stonework and similar places. It is collected and kept fresh in a bucket of water to be used by draping a little over the hook and float fishing it at about mid-depth. Silkweed appeals to roach and chub, less often, dace and barbel too. Most of the success I have had with silkweed has been experienced on hot days during low-water conditions.

Slugs

A deadly bait for big chub, legered or freelined. The brown slugs with orange frills catch fish, but the smaller black slugs which creep river banks on damp mornings are even better. Slugs are sticky creatures and should be handled as little as possible. The cleanest way is with a pair of tongs made from two lengths of wood to which strips of rough sand-paper have been glued.

Wasp grubs

Superb late-summer bait float fished for roach, dace, chub and barbel. During August–September is the period to search for nests. Once one has been located, cyanide should be put down at its entrance to kill the wasps. Twilight is the time for this, when the wasps are back in the nest and least active. On the following day the nest can be dug out and baked to toughen the grubs held within. Baking is simply accomplished by putting the nest in a container placed inside an outer vessel holding boiling water and simmering it there for a short spell.

Worms

Lobworms can be collected in quantity in return for a little after-dark hunting. All that is required is a torch with a subdued beam, a bag or tin to hang round the neck, and access to a close-cropped lawn or verge. Shortly after full darkness lobworms come to the surface and lie half out of their holes. By stepping lightly, shining the torch a little way ahead, the shiny bodies of the worms can be spotted in the grass. To make a capture, first make sure which end of the worm is which, and then grab it at the point where it enters the ground, trapped between finger and thumb. Do not pull too hard or the worm will break. Maintain a steady pressure and as the worm is felt to relax its grip draw it slowly clear. Many worms can be gathered this way in less than an hour, but never take more of them than absolutely needed.

Lobworms are fished whole, in sections, and as bunches of three or four, legered, freelined and float fished. To be really effective bait a lobworm must look right on the hook. It is not much use jabbing 12 in (30 cm) of worm back and forth through its body until it resembles a sticky brown lump rather than the fish-appealing creature it was

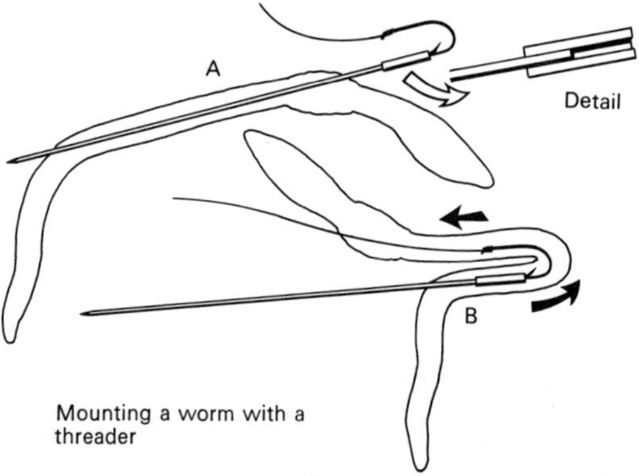

Mounting a worm with a threader

before. A threader gadget designed by big-fish hunter John Stadon is a boon for attaching lobworms properly. It can be made in a few minutes from a 4 in (10 cm) baiting needle and a ¼ in (6 mm) length of metal tube of slightly larger diameter than that of the needle. The needle's eye is snipped off and in its place the tube is pushed on and pinched firm so that half of it remains hollow.

To thread a worm the point of the needle is inserted into the thick band of skin called the saddle and carefully pushed down the inside of the body for several inches before being brought out again through the side. The hook-point is then pushed into the tube's hollow and the worm eased gently up the needle, round the bend of the hook and along the line until the needle is free. This treatment fixes the worm, leaving just the hook-point exposed to the bend and the line coming out of the saddle. The worm is firmly attached for casting but at the same time alive and full of attractive movement.

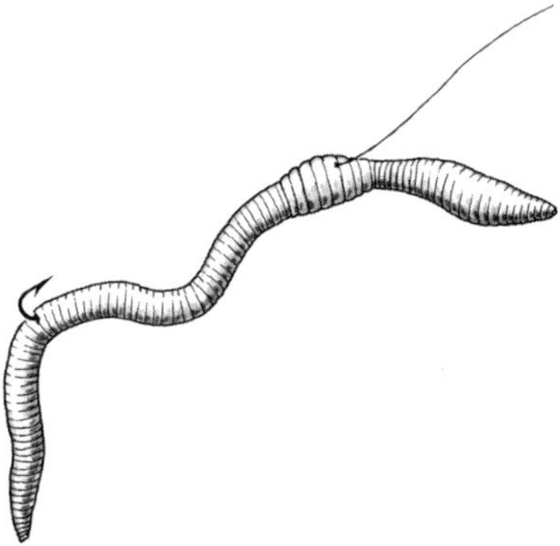

Worm bait

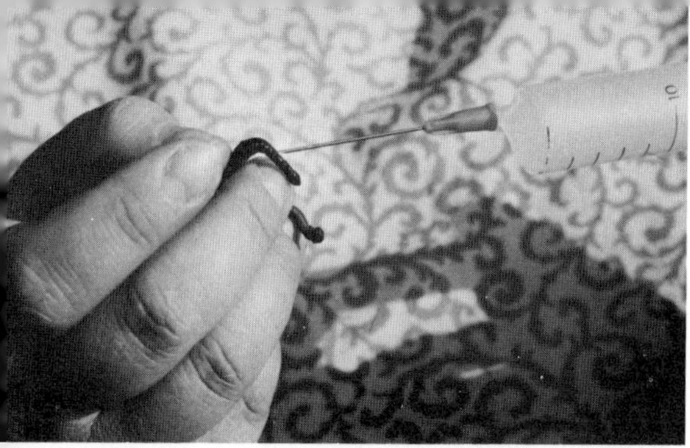

Air-filling a lobworm with a hypodermic needle

To make a lobworm float, inject several segments with air through a hypodermic needle. If only the head end is air-filled and the hook inserted at the other end, it will half-float—the tail waggling the hook enticingly sub-surface.

Smaller worms, brandlings, redworms and gilt-tails, found in dung heaps, under old sacking, lawn mowings, leaves and stones should also be tried as bait.

Worms require no special preparation. New

Baits: maggot (A), caster (B), elderberry (C), hempseed (D), pinched bread flake and maggots (E), caddis larvae (F), silkweed (G)

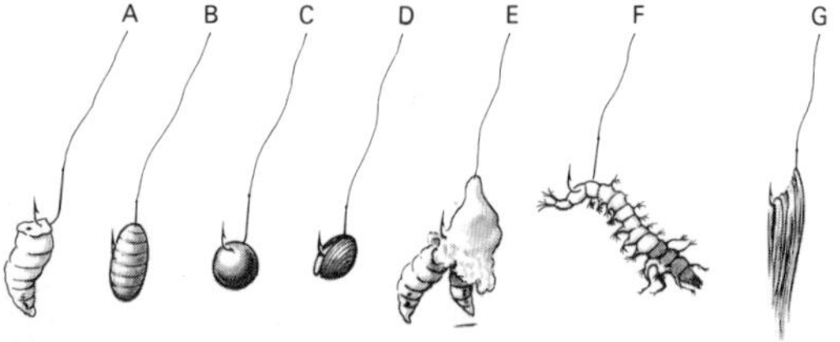

from the ground, retained in damp moss, grass or loam, they remain lively for several days at least.

Groundbait

To gather fish to the area of water being fished (the swim) and to encourage those already there to feed, groundbait is introduced. This is done at the start of a session and then at intervals. For some species (e.g. carp, tench and bream) groundbaiting pro-

Frying-pan baitdropper

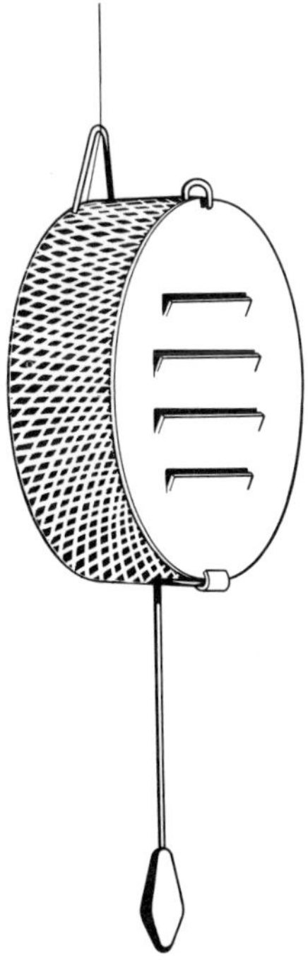

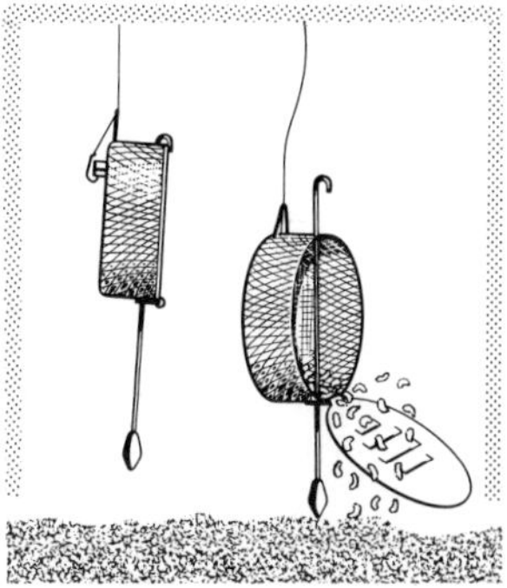

grammes are undertaken lasting several days or longer before the spot is actually fished. Pre-baiting is not always a success, but it does produce satisfactory results often enough to make it a worthwhile proposition prior to the start of the season for anglers living close enough to the water who can get permission to do so.

Groundbaiting at its simplest is the introduction of hookbait samples such as handfuls of maggots, paste balls and chunks of floating crust. To get hook samples down fast in deep lakes and river swims where the current is swift, a baitdropper is used. This device, attached to the end of the line, has a compartment for filling with hookbait which opens on impact with the bottom. A popular design is the frying-pan baitdropper. It is attached by passing the hook through an eye situated at the top of the pan and sticking the point of the hook in a cork block at the back. The baitdropper is swung out underarm and as it falls a catch lifts on contact with the bottom to open the flap. A baitdropper should never be used with a fragile rod as it will impose too severe a strain on the tip section. Other types of hook-sample distributors include specially designed catapults and throwing sticks for long-range baiting.

A throwing stick is a device used to throw light-weight hook samples far out from the bank. A length of bamboo, metal or fibreglass tubing is all that is required to make this item of tackle. A wooden plug is glued 4 in (10 cm) inside one end, and it is in the compartment so formed that bait samples are placed, maggots, stewed wheat, etc. A throwing stick is wielded at arm's length with a firm movement of the forearm and a final flick of the wrist. With practice it is possible to bait-up at fairly long distance very accurately indeed with this

useful piece of equipment.

One way of naturally groundbaiting a river swim is described as 'raking the bed'. For this method an ordinary garden rake is employed; the plan is to wade out well above the swim and rake the sediment and gravel enough to send down a flow of particles and food creatures dislodged from the bottom. This is a reliable means of getting a dace shoal feeding when the river is running low and crystal clear.

Cloudbait is a fine white groundbait which, as its name suggests, clouds the water, attracting fish but not over-feeding them. Its use is largely restricted to stillwaters and canals.

Stodge groundbaits are used when fishing for bottom-feeding shoal fish (e.g. tench, bream, carp and chub) in order to spread the bottom of the swim with enough food to hold their interest for as long as possible. The deeper the swim, the faster its current, the stiffer the groundbait must be mixed.

Plenty of quality branded groundbaits are available from tackle shops made from ingredients balanced to suit every kind of water and situation. Follow the mixing instructions on the bag, adding hook samples, and you will find most of these groundbaits satisfactory.

Here are a couple you can make yourself:

Cloudbait
Fine sausage rusk or breadcrumbs, well soaked.

Stodgebait
Coarse sausage rusk, mixed with either branded *Pomenteg* groundbait or chicken meal.

Hookbaits are carried in various plastic bait boxes. It is important that maggot containers have well-perforated lids to prevent the maggots sweating and turning sour. Large plastic buckets are used for mixing groundbaits and carrying livebaits, etc.

The angler's catapult

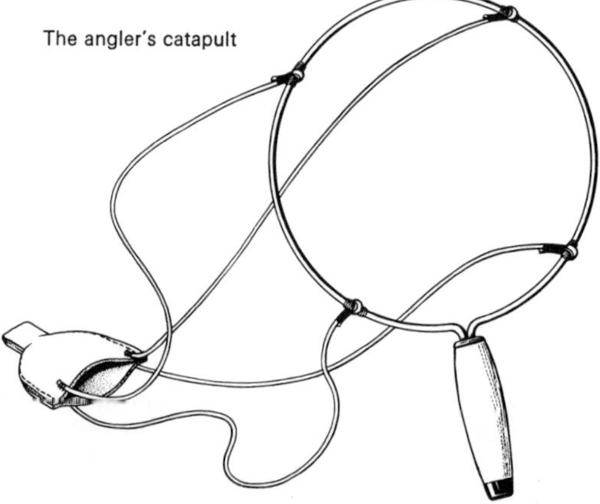

Margin fishing

Freelining Methods

Freelining is a term covering methods in which the line is weightless apart from a baited hook, or a wire trace rig in the case of pike, zander and eel fishing.

Margin fishing is a simple form of freelining which catches carp at night. Carp patrol the margins of lakes during the hours of darkness and by listening for the slurpy noises they make, sucking food from the surface, their movements are tracked and a floating bait lowered ahead of them.

Margin feeders can be stalked along the bank. An easier tactic is to remain in one place and wait for them to come to you. Put the rod in rests with the tip poking out over the water and a crust or air-filled lobworm bait on the surface directly beneath. The line should be slack but held clear of the water.

If fingerling rudd or roach make a menace of themselves nibbling crust bait off the hook, pull the bait up an inch (2·5 cm) clear of the water and lower it down only when a carp moves close by.

Rod and line strength is measured according to the size of carp in the lake and a consideration of snags and weedgrowth in the area being fished. A matchbox-size crust or large lobworm on a size 2 hook makes an ideal duo at the business end.

Roach, rudd, bream and tench are other fish which feed in the margins at night. Providing big carp do not inhabit the water, tackle strength can be scaled down to catch these smaller species.

Try bottom-fished baits as an alternative to floating baits.

Freeline casting requires heavy baits such as wetted crust, potato and paste-ball. Again the rod is placed in rests, but now with a loop of line pulled down between reel and first ring held by a bite-indicator. For carp the bale-arm of the reel is left open to give line freely—a wise precaution because carp frequently run with the bait at great speed.

Silver foil bent tube-shape over the line is a good indicator. It is important that the tube is at least 3 in (7·6 cm) long to overcome line twist and the possibility of a line-breaking jam at the butt ring

With the bale-arm open a running fish takes line freely

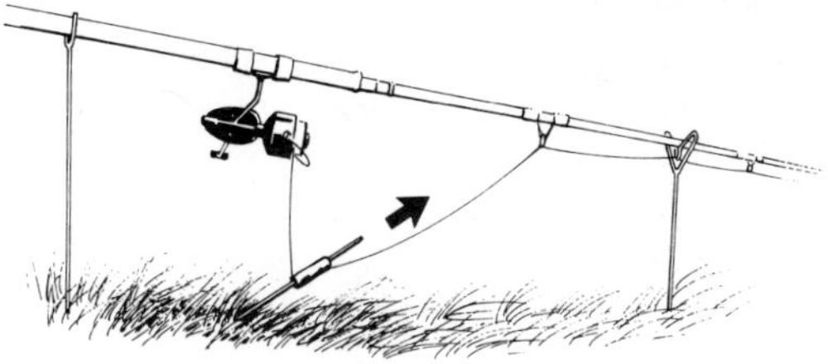

Knitting needle method of holding a tube indicator

as a fish runs out line. In windy weather, lightweight indicators need greater securing to stop them swinging about giving false bite indications. A method of doing this with a foil tube is to stick a knitting needle in the ground beneath the rod pointing directly towards the butt ring. The tube, mounted on the line, is pushed over the needle. When a bite occurs the tube is lifted clear.

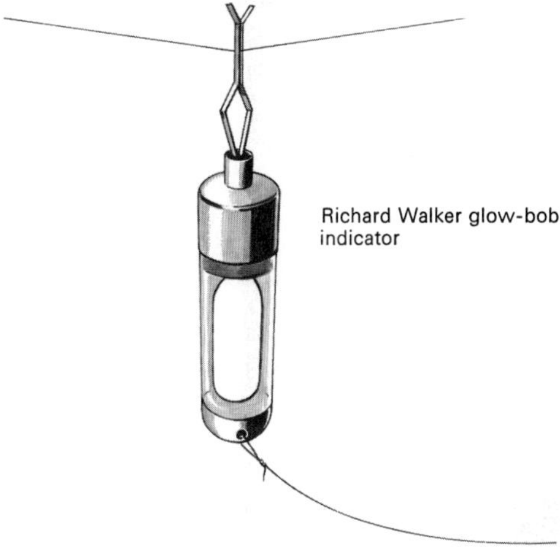

Richard Walker glow-bobbin indicator

Electric bite indicators. (*above*) The buzzer-only 'Watchman' indicator. (*right*) The Pegley-Davies 'Red Alert' fitted with a buzzer and a light. Its indicator head screws on to the end of a bank stick

Electric indicators fitted with lights and buzzers are used for carp at night. Glow-type indicators for other species. A glow indicator, such as the Richard Walker glow-bobbin, should be secured to the back-rest by a length of thread so that when flicked off on the strike it will not be lost in the foliage or water.

Fish lily-beds during hot summer afternoons. Carp seek these spots for food and shelter, and they can be enticed to take a freelined floating bait tossed to lie in a clear space of water between the pads.

Lily-beds are jungles of stems and roots. Extra-strong tackle is essential: heavy-duty rod, size 2 hook, line at least 15 lb (6·8 kg) test—even when the carp run no larger than 3 (1·3) or 4 lb (1·8 kg).

Strike immediately the bait is sucked under, hold tight, and quite literally drag the fish back through the growth. A tug-of-war of this nature is a real test of nerves should the carp hooked happen to be a very big one!

The above methods are also suitable for canals, sluggish rivers and backwaters of fast rivers.

Trotted crust is a productive freeline technique for river chub during the summer months. Gain the interest of chub by sending down the current a few loose chunks of crust. Watch their progress carefully and when they start getting pulled under follow with a further crust chunk on a size 2 hook and 5 lb (2·2 kg) test line. When a chub takes the bait, pause a second or two, then strike the hook home with a firm sweep of the rod. To help keep the line on the surface, spray it with a water repellent (e.g. WD-40 or AP-75) or lightly grease with vaseline.

Freeline pike deadbaits, herring, mackerel and freshwater bait-fish of similar size, in still and slow-flowing waters. Set the rod in rests with the bale-arm off (drum in casting position if a side-cast reel is used) exactly the same as for carp. A main difference is that a pike run is left longer than a carp run before striking to give the pike the time it needs to turn the bait headfirst into its mouth.

A lily-bed jungle where carp lie during hot afternoons

Deadbait rigs are many, and there is not space to even begin to mention them all. Suffice to describe just one. It is made from a 24 in (60 cm) length of 14 lb (6 kg) multi-strand or nylon-covered trace wire as follows:

First, a two-way swivel is secured to one end of the wire for attachment of the rig to the main line.

With multi-strand wire this is done by taking the end twice through an eye of the swivel and binding it in tight close turns around its main part for at least half an inch (12 mm). Nylon-covered wire is taken only once through the eye, then twisted in open turns along the main part and fused as a hard join by moving a match up and down the twists to melt the nylon covering. This join should be about 1½ in (38 mm) long.

Next, a size 6 long-shank hook is threaded on the wire, followed by two medium size treble hooks. To complete the rig a third treble hook is secured

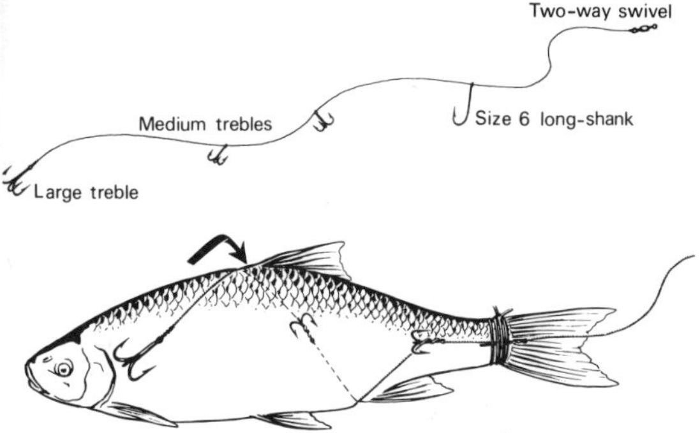

Deadbait rig

to the free end of the wire in the same manner as the swivel was.

To mount a bait, the end treble is hooked in its side near the gill-cover and the wire taken over its back. Here the first of the running trebles receives two twists of the wire before being inserted in the flank halfway along the length of the fish. The wire is then taken under the bait and the same

Hooking positions

process repeated with the second running treble, inserted in the opposite flank nearer to the tail. Finally the wire is twisted several times round the shank of the single hook which is fixed deeply through the tail root to be held in place with a few turns of thread.

Always puncture the swim-bladder of a freshly killed bait or it may fail to sink. For fish of small-herring size make up rigs which have only one running treble.

Freeline pike livebaits from a boat to search

Dapping

deep corners of lakes. Lower the bait over the side, giving line gradually as it swims downwards. A single-treble trace hooked through the top lip or the front root of the dorsal fin allows the bait maximum freedom of movement. (See page 92.)

Dapping live insects in the surface film over the heads of surface-feeding chub, roach, rudd and dace is never an easy method, but nevertheless it produces plenty of good fish from overgrown canals and small streams. The angler must remain undetected by the fish and yet get close enough to them to dibble insects from above. (See page 93.)

Dap insects freeline-style in windless conditions. Add a small drilled bullet stopped by a split-shot 12 in (30 cm) from the hook when extra control is needed. Hook-size for dapping matches the type of insect to be dibbled. Line tests: 3 lb (1·3 kg) for dace, roach and rudd; 5 lb (2·2 kg) for chub.

Stillwater Legering Methods

Leger stillwaters with a link-leger or Arlesey bomb to cast lightweight baits over a distance and to sink buoyant ones. The length of line between hook and stop-shot is called the trail. It is adjusted to suit the bite-pattern of different fish and to present buoyant baits at predetermined depths above bottom.

For example, crust is a very buoyant bait. With a trail length of 2 in (5 cm) it will lift just off-bottom. On the other hand, a trail length of 36 in (91 cm) in 36 in (91 cm) of water will float it on the surface.

Depth versatility of legered buoyant baits is something to keep in mind when fishing a lake.

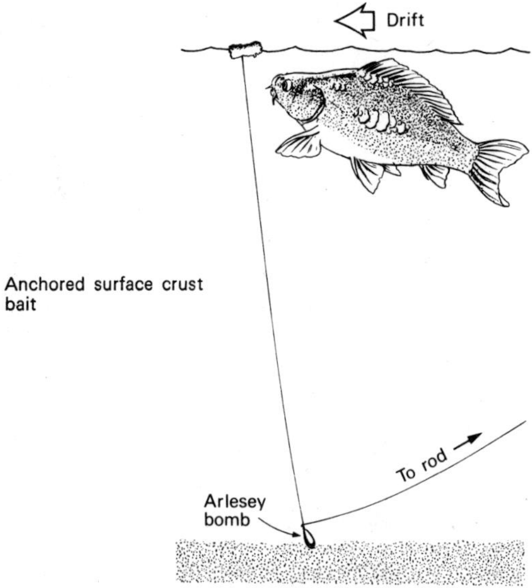

Typical advantages are (1) Over a bed of thick weed a buoyant bait can be suspended above the growth so that it is completely exposed to fish passing by. (2) Surface anchored, a buoyant bait is presented with the line totally submerged—excellent in windy conditions and a reasonable answer to the problem of carp crafty enough to circle a bait before approaching it to make sure it is not attached to anything 'dangerous'!

Eighteen inches (45 cm) is an average trail for non-buoyant baits. Be prepared to make changes when fish give bites which are consistently missed no matter how quickly they are struck at. A trail

A played-out
perch is eased
to the net
(*Bill Howes*)

PLATE I

A catch of fine rudd carefully prepared for photographing (*Bill Howes*)

(*above*) Match fishing the Thames at Walton (*Bill Howes*)

PLATE 2

Concentration, so essential to successful angling (*Bill Howes*)

Weir runs—the home of fish of all species (*Bill Howes*)

(*above*) Tall bankside growth provides the angler with ideal cover (*Bill Howes*)

PLATE 3

(*left*) Carefully extracting the hook from the mouth of a chub (*Ray Forsberg*)

(*right*) Jetty and wood piles—typical haunt of perch (*Bill Howes*)

Peter Butler shows a correct method of weighing fish without harming them (*Bill Howes*)

PLATE 4

With gentle care a hefty mirror carp is returned to the water (*Ray Forsberg*)

A rare golden tench from Woburn Abbey lakes (*Bill Howes*)

PLATE 5

A specimen zander captured by Barrie Rickards (*Barrie Rickards*)

Peter Frost displays a rare catfish (*Trevor Hutchings*)

(*above*) Winter fishing for pike (*Bill Howes*)

PLATE 6

(*right*) A superb 28 lb (12·7 kg) pike coated in the clever camouflage of its species (*Bill Howes*)

Plump and silky, a memorable June-caught tench (*Bill Howes*)

PLATE 7

Vell-known ngler Billy ane with a plendid bag f big roach om the Iampshire von (*Bill Iowes*)

Being afloat can be an advantage when lake fishing for rudd (*Bill Howes*)

PLATE 8

A nicely conditioned barbel held by its captor (*Bill Howes*)

When all has be[en] made ready, fishing is often then a matter of relaxed patience (*Ray Forsberg*)

Bread paste dough-bobbin indicator

variation of a few inches can make all the difference, turning slight pulls and plucks into bold takes.

Rod rests and bite-indicators are used for still-water legering. Reel bale-arm closed for roach, rudd, crucian carp, tench and perch. Reel bale-arm open for common carp, pike, zander, eels and catfish.

Keep the weight of the leger lead as low as possible to cast the distance and to counteract any wind-created surface drift.

The open-end swimfeeder is often employed in place of a leger for lake fishing. It is an arrangement well proven for tench, roach, rudd and bream.

Fix the trail length at 12 in (30 cm), put the rod in rests, and add a dough-bob indicator to the loop between reel and first ring. Leave for a few minutes to allow the groundbait plugs to soften, then bring the swimfeeder back 12 in (30 cm) to expel the contents from the tube in a patch on the bottom with the hookbait right in the middle—the 'hot-spot'.

Swingtips and quivertips are sensitive bite indicators which fix to the tip of the rod. Experienced anglers, particularly matchmen, favour them for both stillwater and river legering.

Left: multi-treble rig for pike and zander. Right: singie hook eel rig.

Leger small fish, sprats, young rudd and roach, etc., for pike and zander on fine-wire traces incorporating two or three tiny trebles inserted along the flank. For eels use a single-hook wire trace, the wire threaded through the bait [a 4 in (10 cm) dead roach] with a baiting needle so that the bend of the hook rests in the corner of the mouth. Micro-fish baits (minnow size) are lip-hooked: to nylon for perch, to fine-wire traces for other predators.

River Legering Methods

Leger rivers to present baits along the bottom. Cast a leger of the right weight downstream and

The baited hook, cast to A, rolls with the current to B

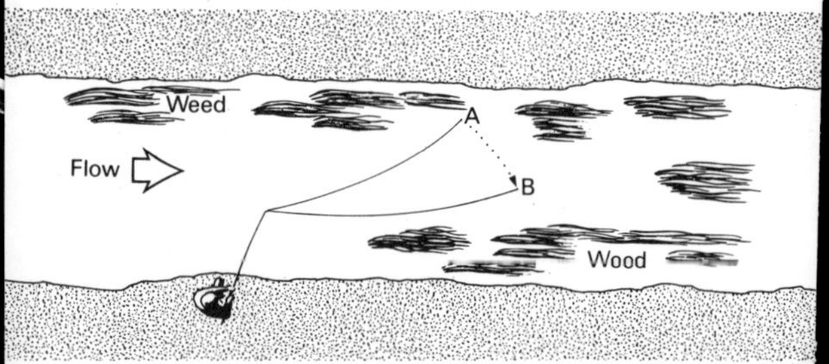

across so that it rolls the bait to a spot where it is judged the fish are most likely to be . . . under the bank further below . . . alongside a clump of reeds . . . in a slack at the tail-end of an island, and so on.

By altering the length and angle of each cast, and by lifting and lowering the rod with pauses between movements, a rolling leger can be made to search every inch of the river bed.

Leger leads used for the rolling technique include Arlesey bombs of ¼ oz (7 g), ½ oz (14 g), and ¾ oz (21 g) sizes and swanshot link-legers. The latter have the advantage of being finely adjustable to meet the needs of many different swims and the varying strengths of current flowing through them.

Upstream legering is a more difficult method than downstream legering but ideal for those clear channels at the tails of large weedbeds which prove awkward to fish downstream. It is equally ideal for catching 'lippers'—chub and roach which lift the bait and tug it hard but fail to take it properly. When legering downstream 'lippers' pull the rod hard over cast after cast, and yet striking merely results in the bait being plucked away from the culprit. Upstream legering means the strike is made downstream, giving greater chance of the hook dragging back into the fish's lip.

An upstream leger lead (link-leger) must just, and only just, hold bottom against a reasonably taut line. When a fish picks up the bait, turning downstream with it, the weight of the leger should be sensitive enough to dislodge immediately, offering no resistance at all. As the line falls suddenly slack, wind the line tight again as quickly as possible and strike. If you are really on the ball

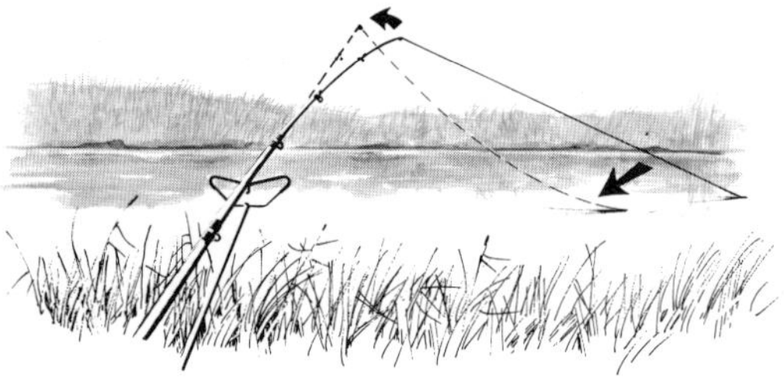

Rod and line falling slack (arrowed) is indication of a bite when upstream legering

you can also be up on your feet and backing away at the same time.

Rod position when legering downstream is at an angle down and across river, with the fingertips of the free hand holding the line above the reel to feel bites. Bites are invariably felt before they are seen when legering with the current so this point should never be neglected. The forefinger of the hand holding the rod rests against the spool of the reel as additional control when striking bites.

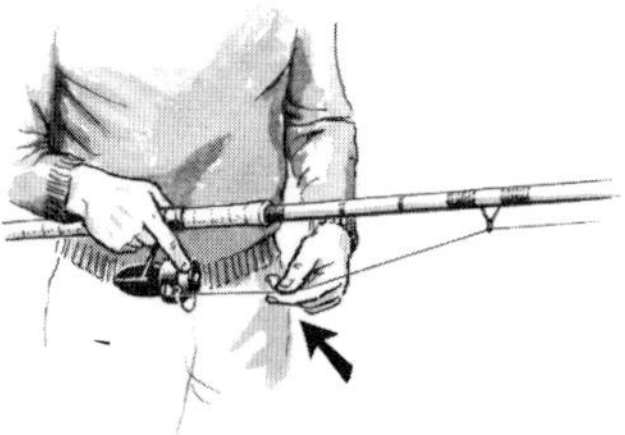

Feeling for a bite

The rod is placed in a long front rest for upstream legering, facing towards where the bait lies with the tip pointing high in the air.

Static legering is required when there is need to cast a bait to a spot in the river and have it remain in position against pressure from strong currents. A case in point is when fish are gathered beneath a stretch of bushes overhanging the far bank, and the current across width is so fierce that a rolling leger bait is carried past them too fast to be investigated. Under such circumstances a swivelled coffin leger lead is used, as heavy as conditions demand. This presentation is not nearly so sensitive as the rolling leger or upstream leger, but used in the right places it still catches plenty of fish.

Legering fish on the outer margin of slacks bordered by fast water is another purpose for the swivelled coffin lead. Deadbaits mounted on the rigs already described. Livebaits lip-hooked on single–treble rigs.

Block-end swimfeeders are an alternative to leger leads. For some species, especially barbel, swimfeedering is extremely productive.

The block-salt weight is used to cast tiny weightless baits long distance—yet still fish them on a free-line. A cube of salt is cut from a block, grooved, and clove-hitched to the line about 18 in (45 cm) from the bait. After casting, the salt cube dissolves within seconds of touching water leaving the bait drifting weight-free. The addition of a split-shot sinks the bait slowly, a calm weather presentation for deep waters where fish cruise at many levels.

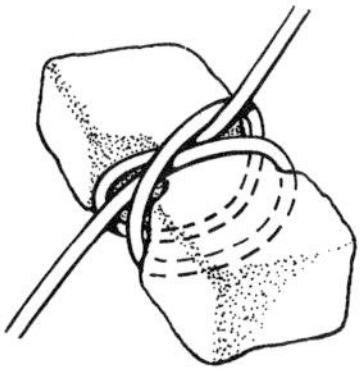

Block-salt casting weight

Stillwater Float Fishing Methods

Quill floats and balsa floats are ideal for fishing swims less than 8 ft (2·4 m) deep during calm windless periods. They are attached with rubber bands top and bottom, and shotted so that just the barest tip remains above surface.

Space the shot on the line as follows: a big shot at quarter-depth, another of similar size at mid-depth, and two or three smaller ones spread out below. By moving the distance of the bottom shot from the hook, the rig can be adjusted to indicate bites clearly; a difference of an inch (2·5 cm) or less is sometimes enough to transform shy dips and trembles on the tip into firm pulls which plunge the float right under.

Depth setting (float to hook distance) puts the bait either on the bottom or off-bottom to suit the habits of the species fished for.

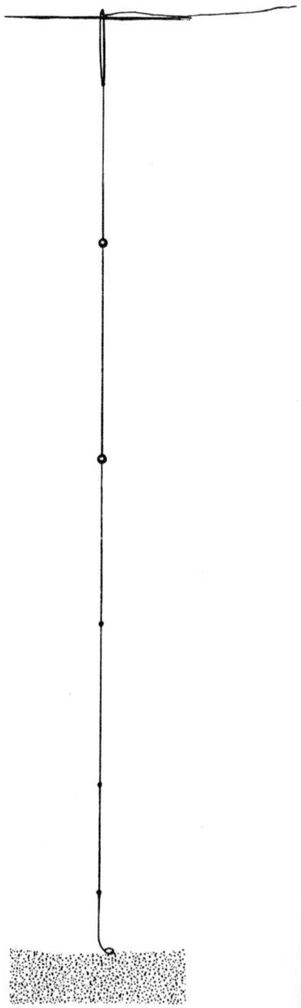

Shotting lay-out

Float size is selected for casting distance. A near-bank swim can be fished easily with a small lightly-leaded float but a swim further out will require a float big enough to carry the amount of shot necessary to cast a bait that far. To counter surface drift, the line should be treated to make it sink by pulling it through a synthetic mud ball of fuller's earth mixed with detergent and a little glycerine.

The lift-method is an important technique for near-bank fishing. The tackle consists of a short length of peacock quill attached by a rubber band at the bottom end and a single large shot pinched on

Lift-method

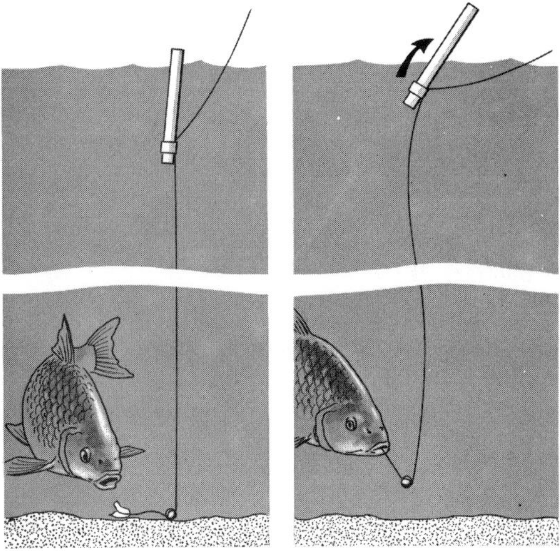

2 in (5 cm) above the hook. Depth is set greater than the water, and after over-casting the swim the tackle is drawn slowly back until the float cocks upright. The rod must be placed in rests for this ultra-sensitive style of fishing.

As a fish sucks the bait upwards it also lifts the shot. The float rises and starts to keel over. Strike as the float 'grows' through the surface and before it has time to lie flat.

This method was perfected for tench fishing by Fred J. Taylor, but it works just as well for other species. It can be scaled up or down according to how shyly the fish are biting.

Antenna floats of small size with long stems and balsa bodies are used for fishing swims exposed to soft breezes. If conditions are not too bad the line is simply threaded through the bottom ring and held in position with plug-stops either side of the ring. For stronger breezes a dust-shot is pinched on above the float to sink the line away from the influence of surface drag. (See page 105.)

Windy weather floats are larger antenna-types. A well-known pattern, called an onion, is a crowquill fished upside down with the addition of a short cork body placed low on the stem.

Shotting these floats correctly is a task which should be taken care of at home to save valuable fishing time. This can be done in a bath or rain barrel by attaching a short piece of nylon to the ring and pinching on the amount of lead desired below the float plus an extra dust-shot. Twists of lead wire are added to the stem directly above the ring to cock the float leaving 1½ in (3·8 cm) of tip above the surface. Pre-test shotting is best left attached to serve as a reminder of the exact shot necessary to balance the float perfectly.

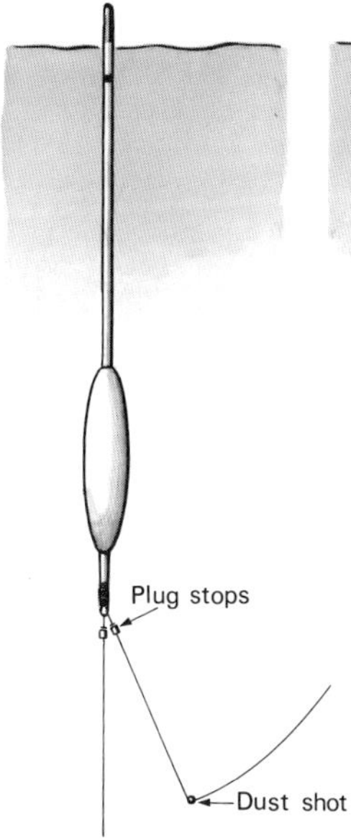

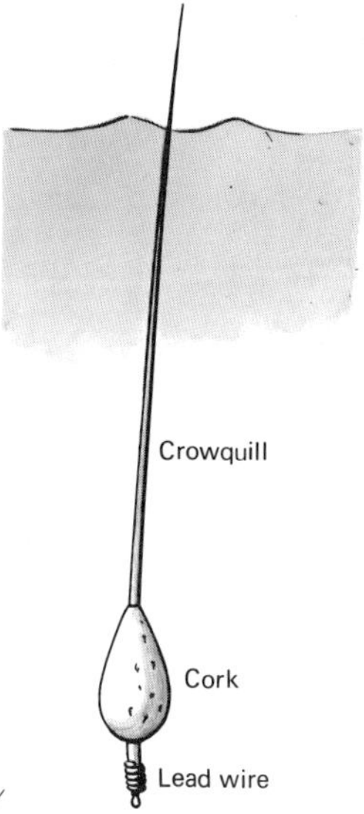

Antenna float rig

Crowquill onion float

To make the rig, a plug-stop is fixed on the line. The line is then threaded through the ring of the float and a hook is attached. All shot go on the line beneath the float, apart from the dust-shot which is added 12 in (30 cm) above the plug-stop as a line sinker.

A typical windy weather float in my box balances a swanshot and an AAA size shot. The swanshot is set at mid-depth and the AAA shot either just off-bottom with a 12 in (30 cm) tail or right on the bottom with a shorter tail of 6 in (15 cm).

The float has freedom of movement between top-shot and plug-stop—the plug-stop being positioned to mark depth setting. During casting the float rests against the shot, sliding up-line as the tackle settles in the water until it meets the plug-stop.

Deep water floats are antenna-types with a large shot-carrying capacity fished slider-style in water where the depth approaches the length of the rod or is deeper. To fish a deep-water slider it is essential to understand how to tie Billy Lane's special stop-knot. It is made from a 6 in (15 cm) piece of nylon in this manner.

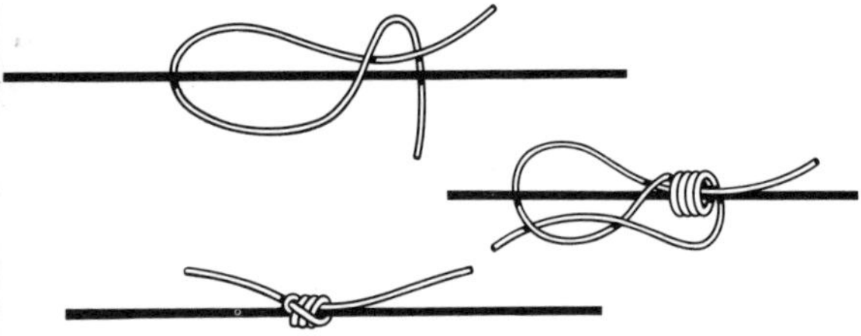

Billy Lane stop-knot

Points to note about the knot are: (1) It must be pulled really tight. (2) The ends should be trimmed off not less than 1 in (25 mm) long. (3) Tied correctly, it moves when the line is tight but holds position firmly when the line is slack.

To rig slider tackle the line is threaded through the ring of the float and the hook is tied on. Shotting consists of a top-shot 5 ft (152 cm) from the hook, a bottom shot 1 ft (30 cm) from the hook, and

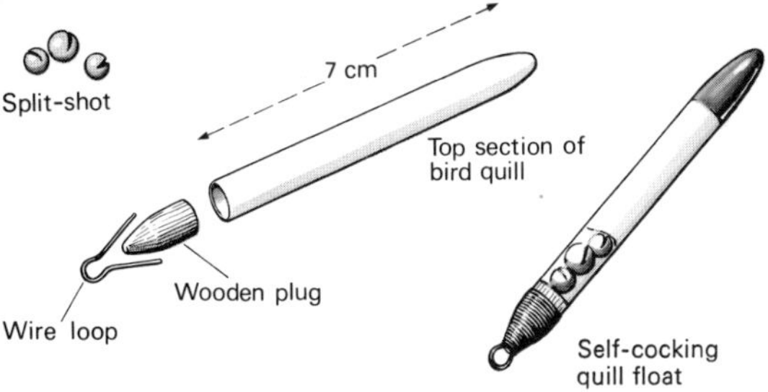

in-between, at 4 ft (1·2 m) from the hook, the remainder of the shot grouped together. A stop-knot is whipped to the line at the estimated depth, and by trial casting with a plummet the exact depth is discovered—setting the stop to either hang the bait an inch (2·5 cm) clear or to have the bottom shot brushing the lake bed.

Self-cockers and semi-cockers are floats which carry weight in their bodies. They are usually attached bottom-end only, for presenting slow-sink baits to upper-level feeders like rudd and dace.

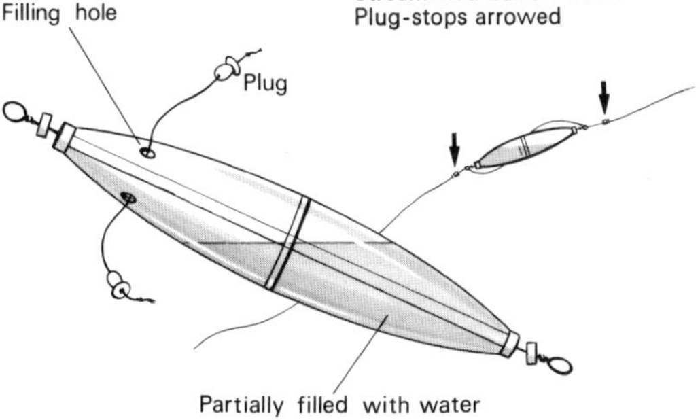

Streamlined bubble float. Plug-stops arrowed

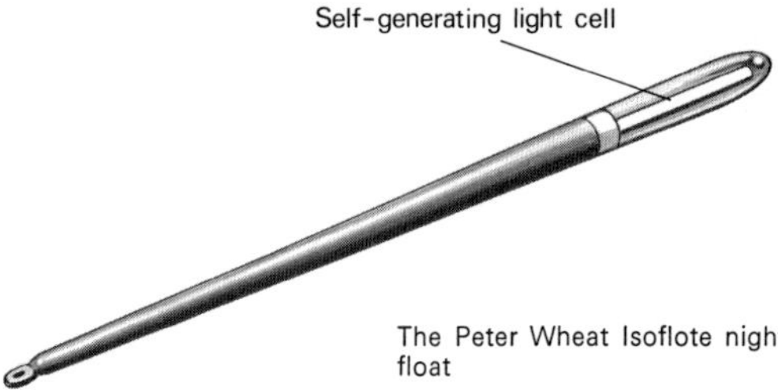

The Peter Wheat Isoflote night float

Bubble floats are either round or torpedo shaped, transparent, designed to be part-filled with water to give weight. They are used in a number of ways but chiefly as a controlling aid when fishing surface baits. They are held in place on the line by plug-stops placed one at each end.

The Isoflote is a float with a self-generating light cell (Betalight) in its tip for night fishing. In shape,

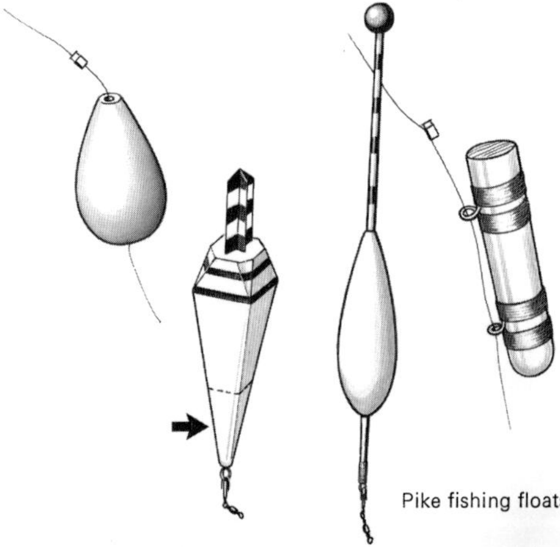

Pike fishing floats

size, weight and shot capacity it is closely similar to a balsa float of about one swanshot size. It can be seen at a range of 10 yd (9 m). An Isoflote is expensive to lose, so the hook-length *below* the float should be 1–2 lb (450–900 g) lighter than the main-line. It will break, without loss of the float, if the hook snags the bottom or up a tree.

Pike floats for stillwater and river fishing include the following. (See page 108.)

Left to right, a drilled cork bung, a self-cocking float made from a Dutch gar-float (the arrow points to the heavily leaded section of its body), a long-stemmed antenna type, and a slider constructed from a metal cigar tube.

River Float Fishing Methods

With slight modifications, float methods suggested for stillwaters can be used in sluggish canals and the slacker areas and backwaters of rivers. But, for float fishing the runs and glides, a quite different approach is required.

Typical Avon floats

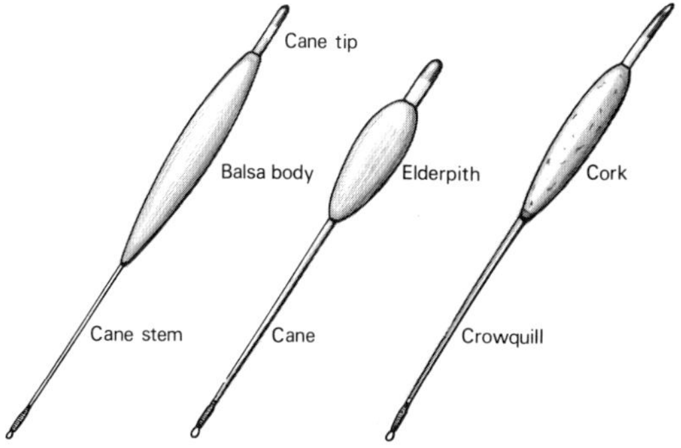

Swimming the stream or trotting involves casting out the tackle with the bait set deep enough to trip bottom, letting it move downstream for a distance, and then retrieving it back to be cast again. When the distance covered in this way is 30 yd (27 m) or more it is described as long-trotting.

For a slow or medium current in water less than 6 ft (1·8 m) deep, large quill and balsa floats fixed top and bottom with strong rubber bands are satisfactory. Deeper, stronger-flowing swims, however, require more substantial floats to take the shot-load needed to get the bait down. These floats, called Avons, have a cane or quill stem and a body of cork, balsa or elderpith.

In very deep swims (e.g. tidal sections of rivers) it

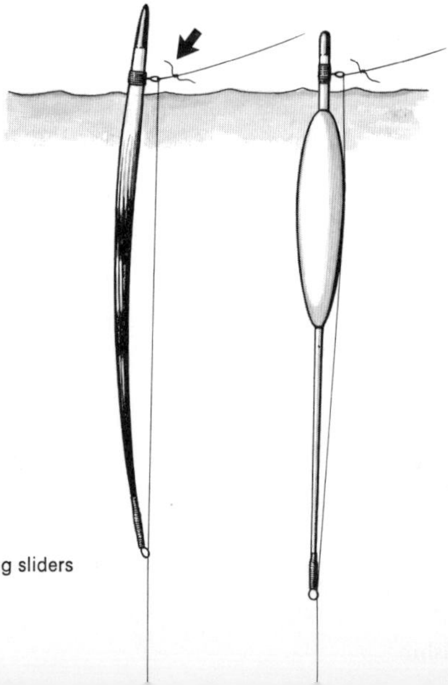

Top-ring sliders

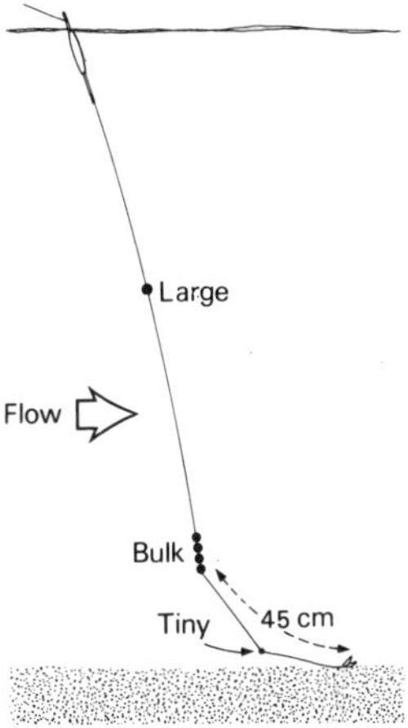

Shotting pattern

may become necessary to use a top-ring sliding float to fish bait along the bottom. The nylon stop-knot is depth-set so that when it is drawn against the ring by the weight of the shot the baited hook will be just tripping bottom.

Always choose the lightest float possible for the conditions, shotted so that about ½ in (12 mm) of tip is above the surface.

The shotting pattern for river fishing is very much a matter of personal opinion. Plenty of anglers like to space the shot out along the line with shot-size gauged smaller and smaller towards the hook. Other anglers, myself included, are satisfied to group the bulk of shot together about 18 in (45 cm) from the hook, and have single shot situated one big one between bulk-shot and float and one tiny one between bulk-shot and hook. The position of the latter shot is adjusted to present the bait as naturally as possible.

The cast is made across river and a little upstream. The bale-arm is then 'turned in' to take up slack and bring the float back into the correct path for moving downstream. All this takes but a brief moment to perform, and then the bale-arm is opened to let line be taken as the float moves with the current. Just how quickly line leaves the reel is controlled either by the forefinger of the hand holding the rod being pressed against the edge of the drum (slow rivers) or by the line passing through the fingers of the free hand (fast rivers). The whole idea is to check the passage of the float enough to keep the tail ahead and the bait bumping bottom.

Sometimes fish lie high in the water and must be angled for with the bait set shallow, but most often it is along the bed of the river where they will be feeding—the larger species definitely so.

Mending the line means correcting the downstream bow which forms in the line by flicking it upstream. There is a knack in doing this without disturbing the float and jigging the bait unnaturally which comes with experience. Careful manipula-

Taking the bow out of the line

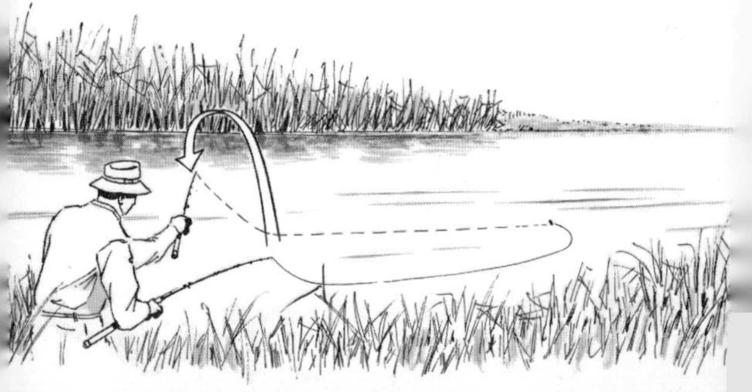

tion of the rod is needed to lift line from the water and mend the bow, but it is important that this is carried out to keep the line between rod and float straight and thereby allow the float an unchecked passage through the swim, presenting the bait naturally. A bellying line, commonly caused by the float travelling slower than the speed at which the line is leaving the reel, also tends to cushion the power of the strike, particularly when striking at long-range.

Line strength for trotting depends on the type of river fished and the size of fish it holds. A point to remember is that if a big float is to be used, and the trot made over 30 yd (27 m) of water, it is vital that a strong line test is selected, even for roach and dace. Striking as hard as is needed to set a hook at 30 yd (27 m) puts the line under severe strain, and anything weaker than 5 lb (2·2 kg) test is likely to snap.

Bites when trotting frequently stab the float under fast and decisive, but it should never be thought that the float *must* become totally submerged to indicate that the bait has been taken properly. Other significant signs to watch for include: the float lift-

A strikeable indication when trotting

ing, the float sinking but not going right under, and the float bobbing off-course from the line of trot. Striking at every movement of the float which looks unusual soon develops an ability to distinguish between the true bites of fish and false knocks caused by the hook dragging bottom or hitting weed.

Striking a bite and getting a hooked fish immediately under control is very easy with the forefinger method; the float dips and instantly pressure is applied to the drum with the forefinger as the strike is made. At exactly the same moment the bale-arm is shut to 'collect' the line from the finger.

When paying out line with the free hand, a bite is connected by holding the line firmly with the fingers, striking, and then passing the line from the free hand to be clamped against the butt by the forefinger of the hand holding the rod. The bale-arm is then turned-in with the free hand to make the final pick-up.

In both cases the drill is extremely fast, and though it may sound awkward and perhaps not completely effective, it is, in fact, perfectly reliable procedure.

Stret-peg a slacker strip of water along the river

Stret-pegging

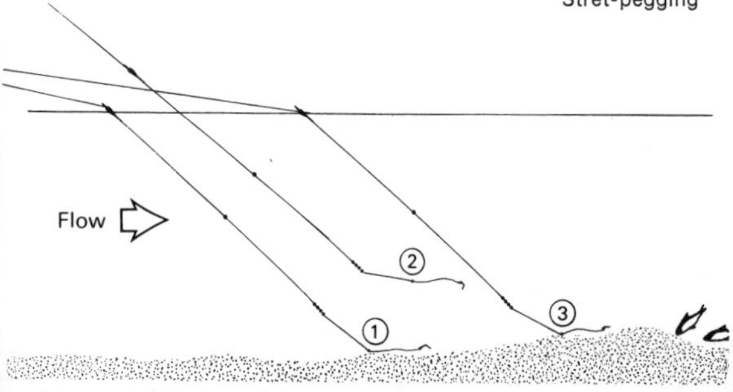

margin by casting downstream close to the bank and drawing the tackle back far enough to straighten the trail right out with the bait resting on the bottom some way below the float.

At intervals of a few minutes lift the rod top high enough to dislodge the tackle, and let out a further foot (30 cm) of line as it is lowered so that the bait reaches a fresh area further down the bank. With inch (2·5 cm) long lobworm sections on the hook this searching method is sound for roach and perch under floodwater conditions. It should be noted that variations in the level of the bottom do not spoil the stret-pegging style of swim searching.

The streamlined bob-float is a handy general-purpose float to have in the tackle box. Its thick shape is perfect for trotting baits in swirly water, rocky shallows, weirpool tails, etc., where many currents conflict. It is especially good for hunting perch, chub and barbel with minnows or bleak as hookbait.

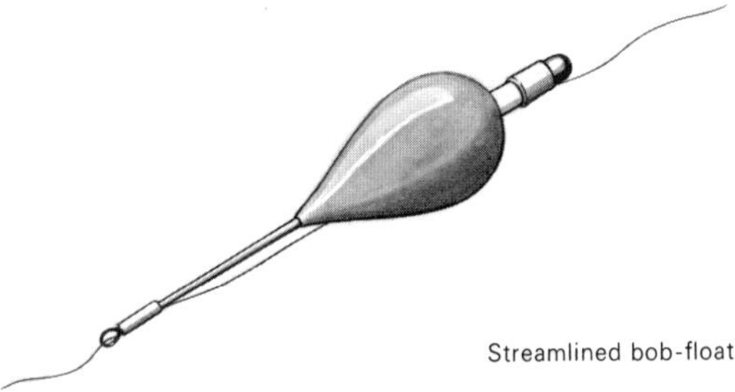

Streamlined bob-float

Fish baits trotted mid-depth in rivers—also canals and drains if they flow—work well for pike and zander. Let the tackle ahead a short distance and then walk behind it for as far downstream as is advisable. Retrieve the tackle and start again from the top end.

Undercut banks, reedbeds and the mouths of bays and inlets, should be given extra attention. Pike love these spots and they 'hole-up' in them fully expecting to make meals of small fish passing by.

Float-tip colours include fluorescent red, orange and yellow. Antenna stems can be seen more clearly if they are striped alternately with bands of black and white topped by orange or red blob-tips.

Completely black floats are, surprising as it may seem, first-class indicators during the half-light period before full darkness. A black float at gloaming can be seen more easily against the silver greyness of the water at this time of day than a float of any other colour.

Floats for shallow water fishing should be matt varnished below the tip. A high gloss finish glinting the sun can scare fish which are moving only a few feet away.

Lure Fishing

Strictly speaking, all hook baits are lures. The term 'lure fishing', however, includes only methods in which baits—artificial and natural—are spun, wobbled, or otherwise worked through the water in a fish-like manner, to entice the interest of predators.

Types of lure include spinners and plugs (artificials), and dead fish (naturals). Many hundreds of different artificial patterns have been devised, to search at every depth from surface to bottom and in some cases adjustable for a range of depths. A few patterns are fitted with anti-snag wires over the treble hook to prevent it catching up in weed. The wires collapse as a fish grabs the lure.

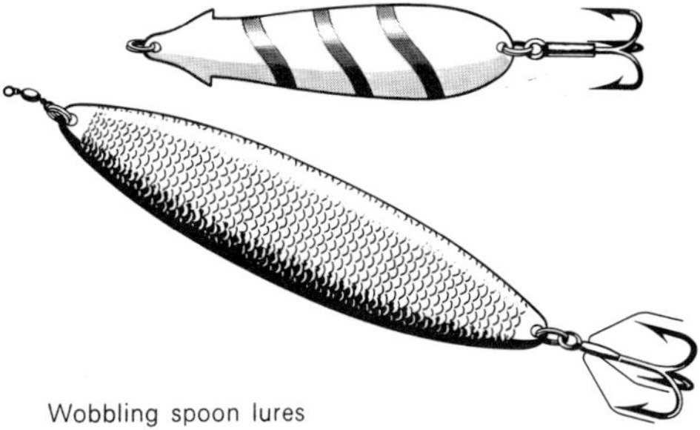

Wobbling spoon lures

Specialist lure-fishers take huge collections of lures to the waterside, neatly arranged in special, multi-compartment tackle boxes. For general angling nothing like so vast an array is required to catch fish and to experience the pleasure of this fascinating branch of the sport.

Rods for lure fishing from the bank should be long, at least as long as 10 ft (3 m), to assist in giving the baits life-like action, as well as to control large fish over the top of snag-filled margins.

An Avon-action rod meets the needs of zander and smaller species, whilst a carp or light pike rod has the additional backbone required to handle the larger fish and heavier lures of pike fishing.

A single-handed baitcaster rod of 5 ft (1·5 m), 6 ft (1·8 m) or 7 ft (2 m) length, is a pleasant-to-use weapon when boat fishing. It has the kind of

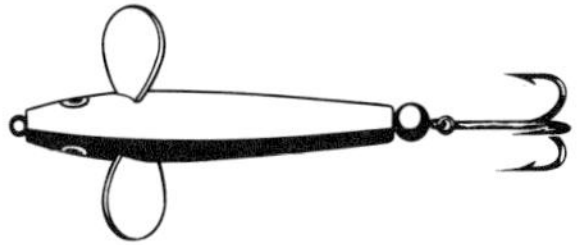

The Devon minnow—a spinning pattern

lively action which makes a 5 lb (2·2 kg) pike feel like a fish of at least twice that weight.

Reels of fixed-spool design are fine for casting lures; the shallow-drum Mitchell range is outstanding. For a crank-handled baitcaster rod a good type of reel is a spincast. This reel, which resembles a closed-face fixed-spool, fits on top of the rod. To cast with it, the thumb of the hand holding the rod pushes down a spring lever on the back of the reel which is released as the lure is propelled out on the forward movement.

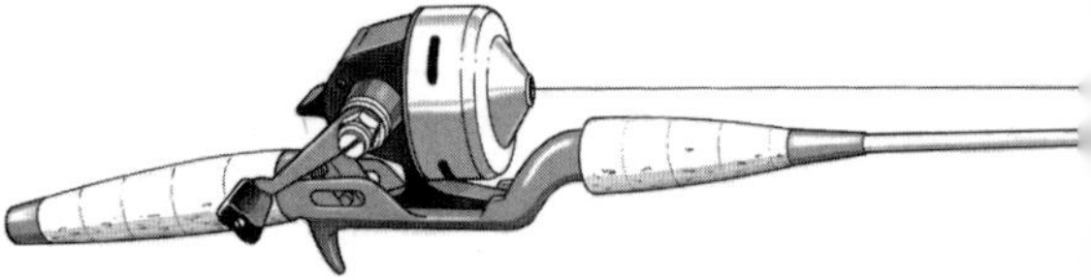

Crank-handled baitcaster rod mounted with a spincast reel

Lines between 3 (1·3) and 15 lb (6·8 kg) test are employed in lure fishing. A choice of strength depends on all the usual considerations: size of fish, amount of snags in the water, and the weight of bait/terminal tackle.

Between 3 (1·3) and 5 lb (2·2 kg) test is average for rudd, perch and chub; 8 lb (3·6 kg) for zander and small pike; and 10 (4·5) to 15 lb (6·8 kg) for big-pike hunts.

Traces are necessary to prevent line twist, caused by a lure which spins, badly fouling-up the line and creating a bird's nest. Length of trace is between 1 (30) and 3 ft (90 cm). For zander and pike it should be wire.

At one end is a two-way swivel for attachment to the main line, and at the other end a link-swivel for quick-change baiting. As a broad guide, the strength of the trace should be equal to that of the main line.

Anti-kink devices further help to prevent line twist by forcing the swivels to turn, which otherwise would not always happen. When light spinning with small baits a plastic anti-kink vane is sufficient. For bigger lures, distance casting, and to get a bait deep down in a strong current, an anti-kink lead is the usual form. The Wye lead, fitted with a link-swivel, and the foldover lead, are common forms.

It will be found helpful at times to use a vane combined with a small amount of lead. Lead is added by 'half-blooding' a nylon tail to the bottom eye of the vane and pinching on swanshot.

All plugs are not fish-like imitations. Some imitate such creatures as frogs and tiny swimming rodents.

Top: Wye Lead. Centre: shotted plastic anti-kink vane. Bottom: foldover anti-kink lead

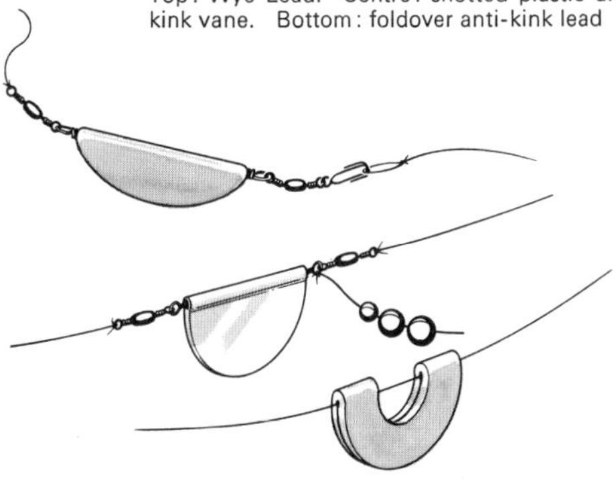

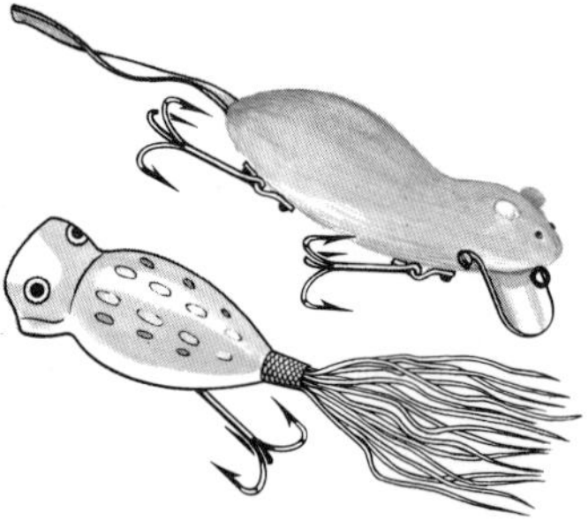

Top: Rodent-imitating lure. Bottom: frog-like surface-popper lure

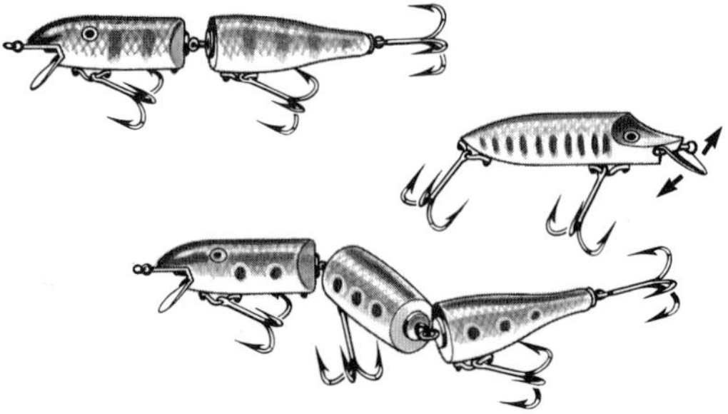

Fish-imitating plug lures. The single-joint model has a lip adjustable to different running depths (arrowed)

Small fish are spun by mounting them on flights. A typical flight, as illustrated, has a paired spinning vane, two treble hooks on short wire lengths and, centrally, a weighted spear. The spear is pushed

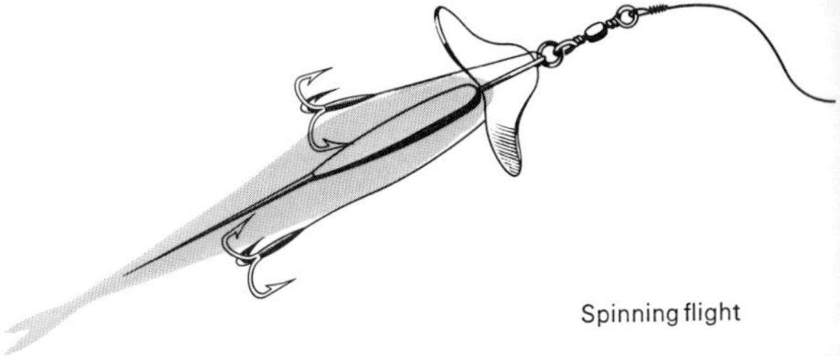

Spinning flight

down the throat of the bait to bring the vane in contact with the bait's mouth, and the hooks are inserted one on each side. To hold everything secure, turns of fine wire arc taken along the length of the bait.

Drop minnow tackle is not difficult to set up. Thread the line through the bait from the tail to the mouth with a baiting needle, add a long-shanked number 6 hook to the end, two or three split-shot nipped on the shank, and pull the hook

Drop minnow fishing

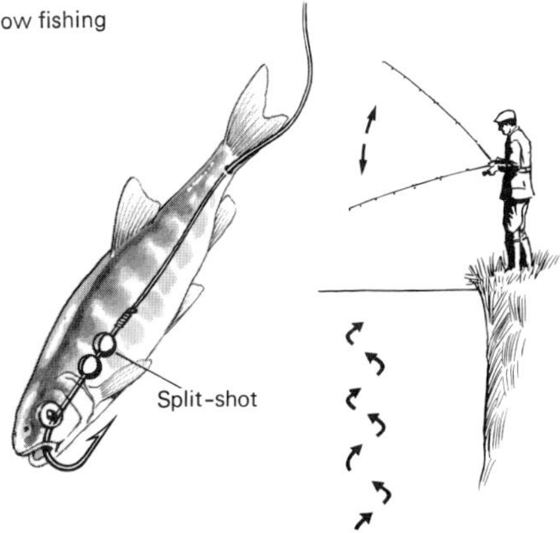

back into the bait until the bend of the hook rests against the corner of its mouth.

Fish a drop minnow for chub and perch in backwaters and sidestreams. Action the retrieve by raising and lowering the rod top to zig-zag the bait along an upright plane. Bring the bait towards the surface slowly, wind the rod down again, and then let the bait fall quickly to the bottom.

Snap-trolling is a sink-and-draw method similar to drop minnow but used with bigger, pike-size baits. The rig for snap-trolling is constructed from an 18 in (45 cm) length of multi-strand wire by adding a barrel lead to one end, threading on two number 8 treble hooks and a single hook, and adding a swivel at the opposite end.

These hooks are held in place by twisting the trace wire three times round each shank so that the points face away from the leaded end, and by binding them over with fine wire. Hooks are positioned to suit the length of the bait: the first treble inserted near the head, the second halfway down the flank, and the single in the tail-root.

Mount the bait by pushing the lead inside the bait's mouth, fixing the hooks, and twisting a few

Snap-trolling rig

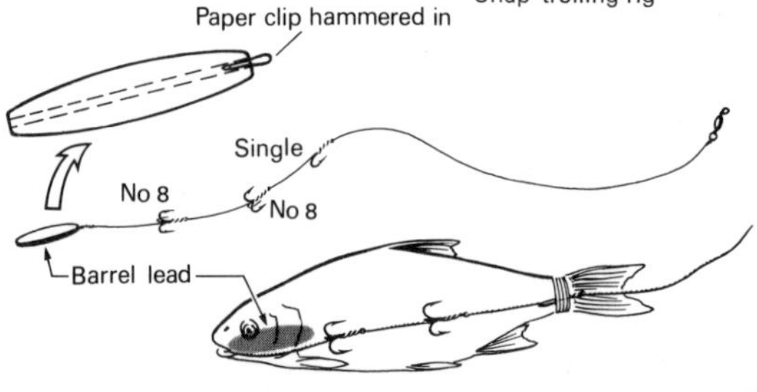

turns of fuse wire at the root of the tail for maximum security. If the mouth of the bait is big (e.g. a chub bait) the lips are sewn roughly together to hold the lead in place.

Holes amid thick weed in stillwater or river, pikey-looking margins and small streams, are places to try with snap-trolling gear. The bait is swung out and allowed to fall to the bottom. Providing the amount of lead for size of bait is judged correctly, it will fall diagonally and move fish-like through the water.

Keep in mind that this is not a long casting method, but an under-the-bank method. Although the bait is mounted backwards it is fished forwards.

Wobbled deadbaiting is a long casting method. The rig is a number 2 treble hook attached to an 18 in (45 cm) length of multi-strand wire. To the eye of the number 2 are trailed two number 8 treble hooks fixed on short lengths of wire—one length a trifle longer than the other.

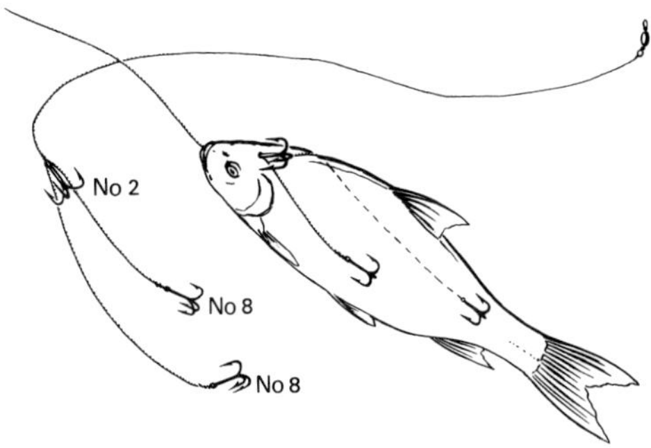

Wobbled deadbaiting rig

Retrieving a wobbled deadbait

The main wire is threaded with a baiting needle from behind the skull of the fish, through and out of its mouth and pulled to bring the number 2 treble hard against the bait's back. Trailing trebles are inserted one in each flank, and a swivel is added in the normal way for securing to the line.

Impart life to the bait by swimming it as erratically as possible with horizontal zig-zag movements of the rod top and sudden changes in speed of retrieve. But never retrieve over-quickly unless pike are feeding really well.

Takes when snap-trolling or wobbled deadbaiting may be felt or seen. Immediately you are aware that a fish has 'latched on', let out a little line, dwell a short pause and strike.

Float-spinning combines a fly-spoon or similar size lure with float tackle. The float is trotted down the stream or cast out across the lake, and then brought back with pauses at intervals to allow the lure to 'hang' in the current (river) or flutter down (stillwater).

Chub and perch respond well to this technique, and so too do lake rudd. Experiment with depth settings. The illustration shows the retrieve action

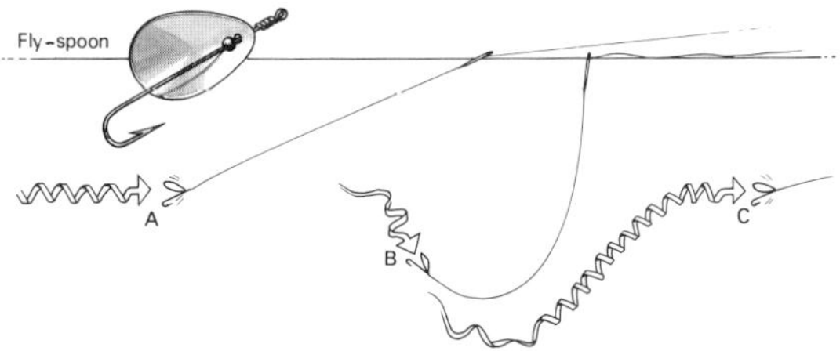

of a fly-spoon being worked beneath a float in a river (A). In a stillwater, a pause in the retrieve (B) sends the fly-spoon fluttering downwards. With the commencement of the retrieve (C) the fly-spoon lifts sharply. This falling, lifting, flashy activity of the lure is extremely attractive to fish-eating species.

The colour of artificial lures is commonly silver or gold, often over-marked with eye-catching spots and stripes. Plugs include patterns outlandishly gaudy and patterns which cleverly imitate the fish which predators feed upon. These, and silvery naturals such as sprats, chub, dace and roach attract predators because, as they are worked, they radiate the flashes and sounds of fish in distress.

Each lure pattern is different in shape, weight and action. And each must be fished in its own way to be effective. Trials with varying retrieve speeds and under differing weather conditions are always worthwhile experiments. Some lures attract fish better on dull days, while others are just as productive on bright days. It is all a matter of trial and error to find out which should be used when.

Above all, when fishing a lure, try to imagine its passage through the water. Make it move as a fish does as far as possible—either wounded, or as a bold invader of a predator's lair. Pike attack lures not only for food, but also because they get annoyed when strange creatures keep buzzing past their noses!

A pike of 10 lb (4·5 kg) taken on a silver wobbler lure

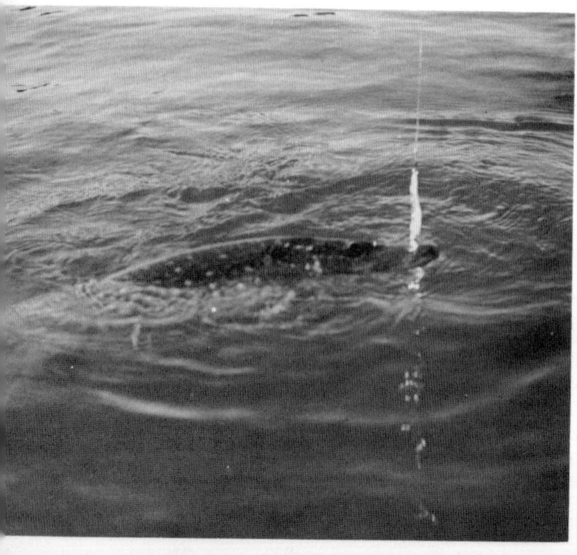

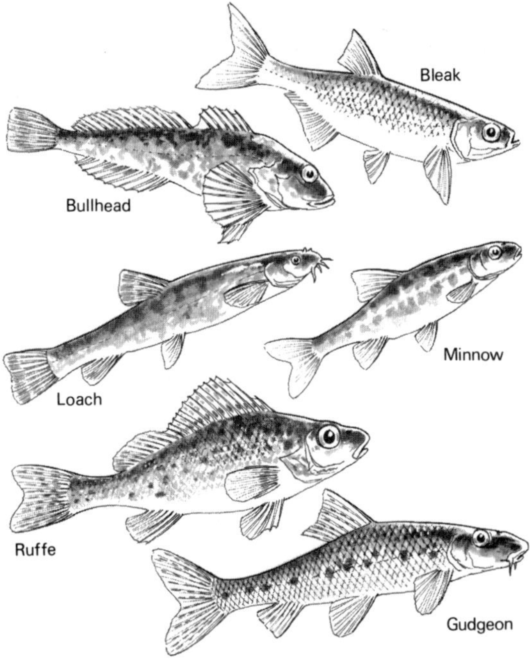

Bait species

Bait Fish

Bait fish are fish which do not grow large enough in themselves to be a sporting proposition, but which can be used on the hook to catch other, more interesting species.

Bleak: Common fish in some rivers where they form vast, greedy-feeding shoals. Easily caught in quantity with fine float tackle and maggot bait set between mid-water and surface. Bleak average no more than an ounce or two (28–56 g).

Gudgeon: Another fish weighing only a few ounces. Gudgeon are bottom feeders. They occur in lakes, but more frequently in swift-flowing rivers. To be caught by float fishing baits of worm and maggot close to the bottom. Groundbaiting and raking the river bed will quickly encourage a shoal of gudgeon to feed.

Ruffe: A localized river species rarely exceeding 4 oz (113 g) weight. In rivers where they occur (e.g. Thames) they are really a lot harder to avoid than to catch in any slack or slow run which has become their home. Worms are bait enough; lightly legered or float fished.

Telescopic minnow trap

Minnow: The smallest of the bait fish, widely distributed in rivers. Most easily taken in quantity with a minnow trap—a telescopic container with an entrance designed so that fish can enter without trouble but find extreme difficulty in getting out again.

Minnows (and fry of other species) are attracted to the trap by baiting a chunk of bread inside it. The trap is lowered down the edge of the bank or on a gravel shallow where minnows are congregated. It should be angled on the river bed with the entrance hole facing into the current.

When several minnows have become imprisoned, the trap is lifted and the captives transferred to a water-filled bucket or thick plastic bag. (See page 127.)

Loach and Bullhead: Two species found in brooks. Collect by wading with a net upstream searching weedbeds and beneath stones. Fished dead, legered or freelined, these tiddlers make grand bait for big chub.

3: PRACTICAL FISHING

On Catching Fish

Coarse fishing is an enjoyable pursuit at any time of the season and in every type of water. But the sport is at its best when it offers a reasonable chance of contact with fish of good average size.

As I write, a roach of 2 lb (900 g) stares down at me from its glass case on the wall. I do not normally kill fish to make trophies of them, but that roach I did keep because it was my very first 2 lb (900 g) roach and as such a significant milestone in my angling life. I caught it by long-trotting double-maggot down a glide of Hampshire Avon towards the close of a November day when most of the other fish which had come to the net had been chub.

Extra big specimens are often hooked 'out of the blue' like that, when least expected. And this being fact it would be quite untrue to say that an element of luck does not play a part in successful angling.

The aim of the game is to reduce this need of luck. One should constantly strive to improve knowledge and ability, mastering as far as one is able, fishing in the right way, at the right time, in the right places and with the right baits, so that the odds weigh in favour of success through personal effort rather than good fortune alone.

Stunted fish and young fish are easy to catch because their numbers are great and they must eat frequently, continually, to avoid starvation. The instincts of these small fish are relatively undeveloped. They cannot afford to be over-particular about what they will, and will not eat. Their attitude towards baited hooks is suicidal to say the least, and they can be an outright menace when the intention is to catch larger fish.

I shall say no more of tiddlers, but confine my remarks to fish of reasonable size which are an entirely different proposition. Although they also eat—to a greater or lesser extent—all the time, their main feeding periods are much more clearly defined. Such key factors as water temperature, oxygen content, light intensity and food availability, affect the feeding habits of different species in different ways—influencing the depth at which main feeding takes place and the part of each 24-hour period when it occurs.

Each species is unique in its feeding pattern. It is true that some species are so closely akin in evolutionary development that only minute points of feeding indicate them apart, but other species are widely separated: classed as evening–dawn feeders, night feeders, day feeders, 'round the clock' feeders, etc.

Quite obviously many good fish are caught in circumstances which do not make them conform to accepted feeding patterns. It should be remembered, however, that these captures *are* exceptional and in no way relate to the *typical* habits of fish—the habits which anglers need to understand to be successful.

Coarse fishing seems to get categorized into summer fishing and winter fishing—a division rather of weather change than of calendar date.

Just so long as conditions remain mild, summer methods and tactics continue to apply no matter how late in the year. It is not until water temperature plunges, as air temperature decreases and cold winds and rains begin to prevail, that the transition takes place which requires different methods and swims to suit the changed moods of fish living from then on in low-temperature conditions.

All sporting species can be caught during summer months, but in winter not all of them feed regularly enough to be worthy of serious effort to catch them. These dormant species are only ever likely to be caught during the cold months when breaks in the weather bring the water temperature up high enough to stir them back to activity for brief periods.

Extremes of water temperature, high or low, can reduce the feeding of all species to almost nil. For example, during hot, summer afternoons, the temperature of a lake may go up so high and the oxygen content drop so low, that only small rudd remain prepared to feed. In winter, the temperature of a lake may become so far reduced that the whole fish population becomes dormant, unmoving, totally disinterested in feeding. These high–low extremes do not affect river fish quite so noticeably.

Knowing about the effects of weather on fish is information basic to catching them above tiddler size. A point to keep in mind is that once you are able to catch fish of good average size regularly, you can expect to catch extra big specimens occasionally. Moreover, chances of this happening are further increased by specializing for a single species in a water where it is known to reach great size.

Choice of venue is very important. Red-letter specimens simply cannot be caught if they are not in the water, any more than a silk purse can be made out of a sow's ear!

The following brief notes are intended only as an introductory guide to catching the individual species. I assume that fish of good average size (and larger) are in the water, and that it is fish of this quality which the reader desires to catch.

Small Species

Stillwater Roach

Tackle: Avon rod. 4 lb (1·8 kg) line. Size 8 and 10 hooks.
Hookbait: Breadcrust cubes, small worms, sweetcorn, pinched flake combined with maggots—size 10 hook. Whole lobworms—size 8 hook.
Groundbait: A billiard-ball size lump approximately every 15 minutes. Mix groundbait 'tight' and lace with maggots. When legering, mould the groundbait round the lead.
Methods: Float fish on the bottom during daytime. Leger after dark.
Remarks: Roach dislike light. Seek them in deep water and weedbed holes during daytime, and try shallower water at night. Use rod rests and a dough-bob indicator for legering, bale-arm closed.

Strike as soon as the float goes right under (as it lifts for the lift-method) and (legering) when the bobbin is moving smoothly to the rod. Expect to miss bites; stillwater roach often 'lip' the bait without taking it properly.

River Roach

Tackle—for trotting: Float rod. 3–4 lb (1·3–1·8 kg) line.—for long-trotting: Avon rod. 5 lb (2·2 kg) line. Size 8, 10, 12 and 14 hooks.
Hookbait: Breadcrust cubes, pinched flake—size 10 hook. Maggots—size 12 and 14 hooks. Silkweed

—size 10 and 12 hooks. Whole lobworms—size 8 hook.
Groundbait: Little but often. It is most important not to over-bait a roach swim. Throw maggots in as loose feed or put them down with a bait-dropper as additional attraction to balls of groundbait.
Methods: Float fishing and legering.
Remarks: Search the clear channels between the weeds with either trotting tackle or a sensitive leger rig on summer days. Also try silkweed float fished at mid-depth in weirpools run. Come evening, trot open water of slower flow near weed. Should roach still be feeding at full darkness, switch to light legering. A cube of breadcrust static on the bed of a swim where roach night-feed is a tactic which often pays off in the shape of a larger specimen or two.

From autumn onwards, roach gather as vast shoals—to be discovered by long-trotting deeper, smoother runs, where weed has died down. Winter roach fishing remains good all day if the sky is overcast, but dusk to darkness is still *the* period for catching bigger fish. After-dark legering is even more deadly at this time of year than it is in summer. Roach are most happy in a water temperature of not less than 42°F (5°C). Below this minimum they do not feed so actively.

Dace

Tackle—for trotting and dapping: Float rod 2–3 lb (·9–1·3 kg) line.—for long-trotting: Avon rod. 4–5 lb (1·8–2·2 kg) line. Size 12, 14 and 16 hooks.
Hookbait: Maggots and various insects.
Groundbait: Feed the swim with loose maggots and white groundbait. Also rake the river bed above the swim to dislodge small creatures and colour the water.
Methods: Float fishing and dapping.

Remarks: Dace love light. Trot fast water for them on sunny, summer days, and also dap insects along narrow, overgrown streams. Through the winter period dace share deeper water with roach. The sharp difference between the feeding habits of the two species can be noted when fishing swims they share together.

Between morning and afternoon the catch will commonly consist of dace plus a few roach of small size. But by evening, as light intensity weakens, the dace cease feeding to be replaced—after a short lull—by roach feeding as eagerly as were the dace before.

Following a mild winter, dace return to shallow water before the end of February to spawn.

Rudd

Tackle: Avon rod. 4 lb (1·8 kg) line. Size 8, 10 and 12 hooks.
Hookbait: Maggots, worms, breadcrust cubes and pinched flake—hook-size matches bait-size.
Groundbait: Decoy crusts thrown or anchored alongside reedbeds and lily-patches. Maggots and

Crust attractor for rudd

chrysalids catapulted out. For rudd lying deep, small balls of groundbait. When anchoring crusts the best method is to secure them to the stems of rush or reed with strands of water weed. Never use old fishing line or any kind of rot-proof thread as these materials are a deathtrap to birds and animals. *Methods:* Slow-sink, self-cocking float rigs. Margin methods for summer nights. Shotted float and leger rigs in winter.

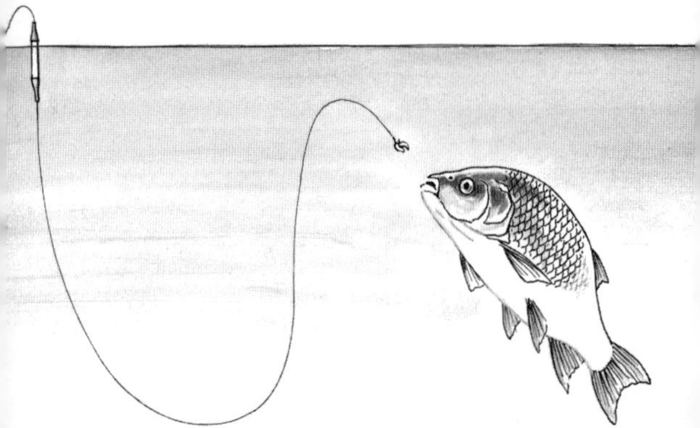

Rudd rig

Remarks: When the weather is warm rudd feed on and near the surface. Once a shoal has been pin-pointed, cast out a slow-sink bait as close to the fish as possible. The float, a self-cocker, should be attached to the line with long, valve-rubber sleeves top and bottom, adjusted so that they protrude beyond the float ends to prevent the hook tangling the float as the tackle flies through the air.

Maggots as bait are an advantage because they cannot be nibbled off the hook easily—something which happens frequently with bread as bait. Worm is a selective bait particularly ideal when large and small rudd are mixed together.

A boat is always helpful. Apart from the increased coverage of the water which being afloat gives, it also enables baits to be cast from angles and distances which makes possible a high degree of accuracy coupled with minimum disturbance of the shoal.

From the bank, a heavily weighted float, 5 lb (2·2 kg) line and a carp rod, may be tackle strength needed to reach the fish.

In winter, rudd move to deep water, remaining near the bottom. Here they seem to prefer baits fished an inch (2·5 cm) off-bottom. Buoyant baits can be legered this distance on a short trail, but non-buoyant baits will need to be cast out on float tackle to achieve the same presentation.

Allow bites to develop properly before attempting to set the hook. The rod is held or put in rests according to how the fish are feeding.

Crucian Carp

Tackle: Avon rod. 3–4 lb (1·3–1·8 kg) line. Size 10, 12 and 14 hooks.

Hookbait: Maggots, flake, maggots and flake combined, sweetcorn, worms and hempseed.

Groundbait: Liberally feed the swim with balls of groundbait laced with hook samples whilst fishing. It is advantageous to pre-bait prior to dusk and dawn.

Methods: Float fishing with the bait on or near the bottom, day and night. Leger only at long range or when the wind is extremely strong.

Remarks: Crucian offer superb sport during summer. They live as shoals in thick weed and beneath lily-pads and these are the obvious places to try for them. Crucian disclose their presence by jumping clear of water and belly-flopping loudly back again, also by sending up patches of tiny bubbles as mud is nosed deeply for food.

Dusk to midnight and first light to mid-morning

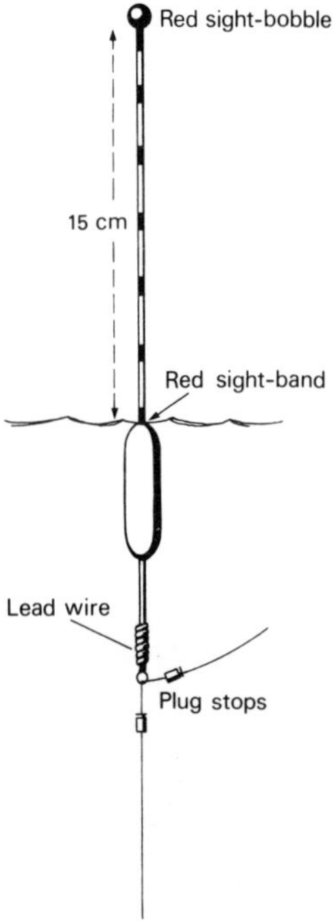

The author's crucian float design

are major feeding periods. They sometimes will feed right through the day if conditions remain warm and dull.

Timing the strike is the most difficult part of catching crucian. The float tours across surface in half-a-dozen different directions, sinking and rising again and again before properly sliding away. It can take as long as five or ten minutes for a bite to develop to strikeable stage—the bait in the mouth instead of held gently between the lips.

Never strike simply because the float is moving. Wait for it to submerge completely or, at the very least, go under as far as the tip.

All my crucian floats are home-made antennas fixed bottom end only, balanced with twists of lead wire at base to cock upright with 6 in (15 cm) of stem above surface. The bait and a single small shot rests on the bottom.

Each float is painted with a red band sight-blob, alternate bands of black and white, and a red band at surface point. The long stem is an excellent interpreter of running bites, and the lower red band an aid in spotting another type of bite which crucian give by sucking the bait in on the spot but failing to run with it. When this happens the float hardly moves; only the red band dips beneath the surface. Should the float sink like this, remaining so for a little time, I tighten the line and strike as soon as the weight of a crucian is felt at the other end. (See page 137.)

A lift rig indicates these delicate-looking bites better but unfortunately is not suitable for dealing with more typical crucian takes.

Crucian become torpid in winter. Should they feed, the bites are generally fast, up-and-down jabs and these fish must be struck without a moment's delay. The rod is put in rests for crucian fishing.

At night an Isoflote float is substituted for the antenna.

Grayling

Tackle: Float rod. 3 lb (1·3 kg) line. Size 12, 14 and 16 hooks.
Hookbait: Worms and maggots.
Groundbait: Loose feed with maggots when maggots are hookbait. Otherwise no groundbaiting is necessary.
Method: Trotting.
Remarks: Grayling are caught winter and summer with trotted baits. They remain active in the coldest weather, and it is then, in the depths of winter, that trotting is most enjoyable. For long-trotting, line test should be increased to 5 lb (2·2 kg).

Grayling are as fond of lying in turbulent waters as in smoother pools, and as the system of fishing is to work the water over, searching many swims of varied depth and character, the float should be thick-bodied—a streamlined version of the grayling-bob float, for example.

Grayling fight with a strange corkscrewing action, made possible by the largeness of the dorsal fin. They use the spread of this fin to such good effect that even quite small fish feel very heavy indeed.

The fight from a 2 lb (900 g) plus grayling remains memorable for a lifetime.

Gilt-tails, cockspur worms, are considered top bait by expert grayling fishers. These worms can be found beneath damp heaps of lawnmowings which have started to rot down.

Perch

Tackle: Avon rod. 5 lb (2·2 kg) line. Size 4, 6 and 8 hooks. Bar-spoon spinners fitted with large treble hooks and small plugs.
Hookbait: Lobworms and small fish.

Groundbait: Perch can be attracted to a swim by cloudbaiting it heavily.
Methods: Freelining, legering, paternostering, float fishing and lure fishing.
Remarks: Perch are opportunist feeders. Summer finds them hidden in thick weed, feasting, as the urge takes them, on fry and small fish. A big perch spotted attacking tiddlers may possibly be caught with a worm, fish bait or spinner, so it is sound planning when fishing lakes noted for perch, but trying to catch other species, to have a spare outfit set up ready for perch should a pack of them put in an appearance. They move mainly at dawn. Undercut banks along clear-flowing rivers sometimes have perch in residence which can be 'teased' to grab a worm freelined or twitched on a split-shot weighted line at first light.

Perch in deep lakes live at the bottom of the deepest parts in winter. Successful methods include running leger and running paternoster rigs

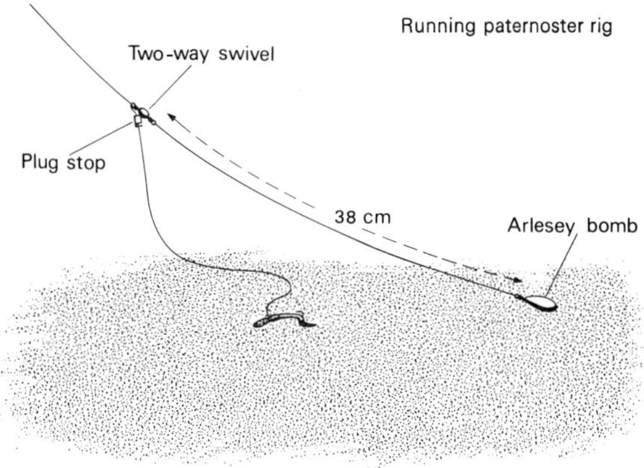

baited with lobworms. The rod is put in rests with the bale-arm left open and a bite indicator such as a tube of silver foil.

Bites need plenty of time to develop. Let line run out without resistance. Do not strike too hard or put too much force against the fish in case the hook-hold is a poor one. It often is with a big perch. Deep-water perch are not fighters and a carefully measured retrieve is all that is required to subdue them.

River perch in winter shoal in slacks, backwaters, mouths of sidestreams and mini-pools formed by reedbeds part-submerged beneath floodwater. Use freelined, legered and paternostered baits in these places. Elsewhere perch take over strips of slow water along the reeds. Any stretch of river which has deepish water under the bank and a reedy margin *may* hold perch. The striped pattern of camouflage which makes perch such showy individuals out of the water blends perfectly against a backcloth of reed stalks, so it is not surprising that in such places they position themselves ready to pounce out and attack small fish which venture close—feeding habits which the worm fisher can take full advantage of.

The approach to the reeds should be softly quiet in order to avoid one's movements being transmitted to the fish. It is also essential to work the float down the edge close enough to the stalks to brush against them.

Different depth settings from mid-water to inches off-bottom should be tried, and changes of bait also. Sometimes a lob-tail will do the trick, while at other times it will be a small whole worm which they want or perhaps a full-grown lob if the mood takes them. Search a section of reeds fully, then move a short way downstream and try again. If perch are at home and feeding they will not need further stimulation than the hook-worm dancing past them.

Strike when the float is carried right under and play the fish firmly away from the reeds—either well upstream or well downstream—for netting. The less the actual perch holt is disturbed the more chance there will be of catching lots of perch.

Middleweight Species

Chub

Tackle: Avon rod. 3–6 lb (1·3–2·7 kg) line. Size 2, 4, 6, 8, 10, 12, 14 and 16 hooks.—Big chub in snaggy streams: Carp rod. 7–10 lb (3·1–4·5 kg) line. Size 2 and 4 hooks.

Hookbait: Bread, maggots, sweetcorn, cheese, worms, crayfish, elvers, meat baits, slugs, small fish and insects of all kinds.

Groundbait: Crust chunks, surface fishing. Loose-fed hook samples, and groundbait balls laced with hook samples, float and leger methods.

Methods: Freelining, float fishing, legering and dapping.

Remarks: Chub are quarry for all seasons. Providing the current strength allows, heavy baits such as slug, crayfish, elvers, bunches of lobworms, and dead fish, can be freelined or light legered in every part of the river system at any time of the year in expectation of chub.

Floating baits—freelined crust, bubble float controlled, air-filled lobworms, dapped insects—catch chub on summer days and warm winter days when these fish will be watching the surface for food coming downstream.

Float fishing and legering with cheesepaste, sausage, bread, worms and maggots as hookbaits,

Strike sequence for 'lipping' chub

takes chub lying in weirpools and streamy runs (summer) and deeper-water slacks (winter). Mild winter spells are opportunity for baiting swims heavily and long-trotting maggots and pinched flake for shoal chub of 1 to 4 lb (450 g–1·8 kg) class.

When the water temperature drops low, chub habitually continue feeding long after other species have ceased. Under these conditions size of bait should be kept small.

Float bites are usually full-blooded enough to slam the float down. Leger bites vary between rod-bending pulls and tiny tweaks not always easy to identify quickly enough to connect with. One type of bite which always presents a problem is the slow take which brings the rod top over a foot (30 cm) or more yet leaves the angler striking at thin air—no matter how quickly he manages to respond.

Bites of this nature are frustrating. They give the appearance of being 'sitters', but in fact are exactly the opposite. The only compensation, at least in my experience, is that chub which produce them are not shy. Quite often they will continue 'lipping' baits cast after cast for a couple of hours at least.

A strike sequence which works is to sit with the rod pointing upriver and across held in one hand, with the other hand controlling a loop of line taken from between reel and butt ring held at arm's length. As a bite is felt this loop is gradually eased out as the fish moves away. Once it has all been taken up and the rod commences to bend, the rod is brought round until it points downstream. As the bend increases the strike is executed. (See page 143.)

Plenty of bites are still missed in this way, but at least enough are connected to prove that giving line is far better than quick-striking when chub are in a playful frame of mind.

Always hold the rod when chub fishing, feeling for bites with the fingers when freelining or legering.

Tench

Tackle: Avon rod. 4–7 lb (1·8–3·1 kg) line. Size 6, 8, 10 and 12 hooks.—For big tench in weedy lakes: Carp rod. 8–10 lb (3·6–4·5 kg) line. Size 6 and 8 hooks.

Hookbait: Breadcrust cube, pinched flake, maggots, flake and maggots combined, sweetcorn, worms, freshwater mussels and meat baits.

Groundbait: Pre-baiting days, even weeks, before the start of the season, is traditional preparation for catching this species. It is a ploy which does not always increase sport, but at least it is an excuse to be at the waterside!

Tench are lovers of weedy areas, and swims are cut from the thickest-grown parts with sharp hook-blades and weed rakes. A good swim-shape is triangular with a narrow channel leading back to the bank. A suitable weed rake can be made quite easily by lashing two garden rake heads back to back with soft wire. Two scythe blades screwed

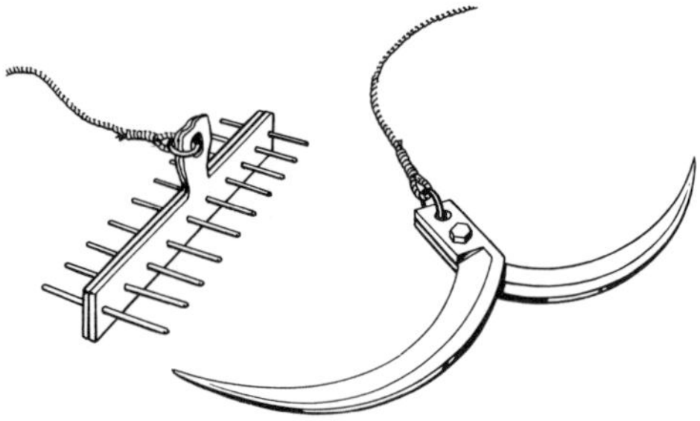

Tools for preparing swims

together make an excellent cutting implement. These tools are attached to lengths of thick cord. They are thrown out, allowed to sink, and then retrieved slowly. By varying the angle and length of each throw the area to be cleared is enlarged to the shape and size required. Great care should be taken when using these tools as careless throwing can lead to a nasty accident. For the same reason double-check that the cord is attached securely.

Tench swims are profusely baited with stodge and hook samples before and during fishing. Raking the bottom at the start of a session, despite the noise and disturbance it creates, actually attracts tench. However, raking should not be carried out if the bed is layered with stinking mud as this has quite an opposite effect to that intended, for obvious reasons.

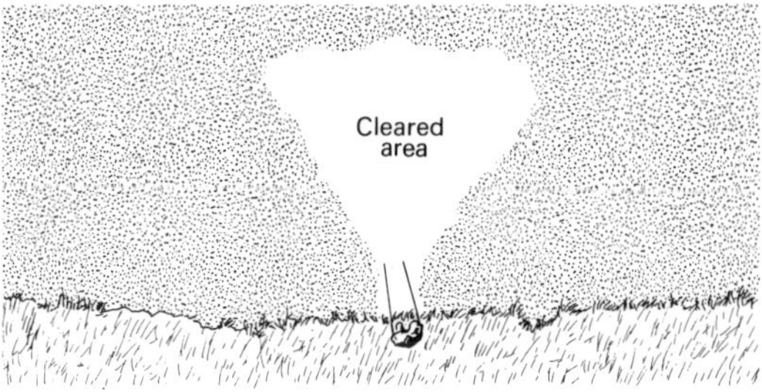

A tench swim located in thick weed

Methods: Float fishing, freelining and legering—particularly legering with a swimfeeder. Swim-feeder legering, with maggots on the hook and in the tube, is regarded as an outstandingly lethal method for tench.

Remarks: Without doubt, tench fishing is most rewarding at the beginning of the season. Indeed, it makes the perfect, dawn-on-the-sixteenth, start and many are the anglers who would not consider any other fish to open with.

By midsummer, tench are difficult to tempt in numbers. They prefer minute forms of natural food to the baits of fishermen. A move to deeper-water swims can sometimes extend the best of tenching longer; tench in the deeps are those which

Bob Church weed dragging a tench swim

failed to move out to the weedy spawning shallows, and among them are hefty specimens of great weight and fighting ability.

Autumn, as natural food decreases, and early March if the weather is mild, are further periods worthy of concentrated tench fishing.

Stillwater tench hibernate, but those in rivers remain active because changing conditions force them to move, using up energy and needing food to replace this lost energy.

A tench bite. The strike is delayed until the float is completely submerged

Tench feed avidly between dawn and mid-morning and between dusk and midnight. Exceptionally, tench continue feeding throughout a day or night. Bites when laying-on with float or running leger tackle are 'sitters' as a rule. The float wiggles, then slides smoothly away; or, legering, the bobbin jumps fast to the butt. Shy-biting tench are common from July onwards, the lift-method being one answer to this development.

The rod is put in rests for tench fishing. Use a dough-bob indicator for day legering and a glow-bob indicator at night.

Zander

Tackle: Avon or carp rod. 8–10 lb (3·6–4·5 kg) line. Wire traces fitted with treble hooks of small size. Spinners and plugs.
Hookbait: Small fish.
Groundbait: Cloudbait—to attract small fish to the swim. Balls of stodge mixed with fish oils and mashed herrings—to attract zander.
Methods: Freelining, float fishing, paternostering and lure fishing.
Remarks: Zander remain active summer and winter. They are peculiar in that they prefer dirty-coloured water to feed in. I believe their marvellous eyesight is a reason for this, coupled with other well-

developed senses. Zander simply find their food easier to catch in coloured water—the very time when other species are most vulnerable to attack. It is probably for the same reason that zander feed at night.

All pike methods scaled down catch zander. They are poor fighters compared size for size with pike though, and for this reason it is important not to use over-powerful tackle.

Barbel

Tackle: Avon rod. 4–7 lb (1·8–3·1 kg) line. Size 4, 6, 8, 10 and 12 hooks.—For sections of rivers known to hold barbel well in excess of 12 lb (5·4 kg) (e.g. middle Hampshire Avon): Carp rod. 8–12 lb (3·9–5·4 kg) line. Size 4, 6 and 8 hooks.

Hookbait: Bread, cheese, maggots, meat baits, hempseed, sweetcorn, worms, crayfish, elvers and small fish.

Groundbait: Large balls of stodge well-laced with hook samples. Maggots and hempseed thrown in loose and put down with a bait-dropper.

Methods: Float fishing and legering—particularly swimfeeder legering.

Remarks: In summer, barbel feeding mainly takes place between late afternoon and early morning. Length of the feeding spells varies greatly according to weather conditions. Later in the year barbel indulge more frequently in bouts of daytime feeding. It is known that barbel in some rivers continue to feed at night in winter (e.g. notably the barbel in the Thames) but more normally the activity of this species after the end of autumn is reduced to spasmodic bursts of middle-of-the-day feeding.

Trotting and legering are methods equally as good for barbel. A choice between the two is made according to which of them is more suited to the needs of an individual swim.

Barbel give decisive float bites. Leger bites vary between gentle trembles (which cannot be seen on the rod but register only through the finger tips) and 'smash takes' capable of dragging an unattended rod into the water. Whether the rod is held or put in rests when legering depends entirely on how firmly the fish are biting.

Eels

Tackle: Heavy carp rod. 10–12 lb (4·5–5·4 kg) line. Size 4 single hook attached to trace wire.
Hookbait: Dead fish—a fish of 4 in (10 cm) is about right size.
Groundbait: Fish chunks and balls of stodge mixed with mashed fish and fish oils.
Methods: Freelining and legering.
Remarks: To bait a dead fish the trace wire is threaded with a baiting needle through the body from mouth to vent before the top swivel is twisted on. The fish is then pulled down so that the bend of the hook is against the corner of its mouth. A split-shot is pinched on close to the vent to retain the bait in this position. Casting weight, if needed, is added in the form of a small, streamlined lead, threaded on the wire before threading the wire through the bait. The weight is pushed deep inside the fish.

Fishing for big eels (nobody fishes seriously for small eels unless they like eating them!) is a pursuit of summer and autumn months. During the day, put out a bait in the deepest water which can be found. At night, when big eels are moving, swims of lesser depth on the edge of deep water should be tried.

The rod is put in rests with the bale-arm open and an indicator attached. Silver foil is a satisfactory indicator for daytime; at night use a bite alarm.

An eel runs with a bait before swallowing it, so allow plenty of time for this to happen. When you strike, hang on tight. A big eel is a fantastically strong animal to tangle with.

Migrating eels weigh between 1½ lb (680 g) and 3 lb (1·3 kg). But eels far larger swim British waters and it is these which big-fish specialists hope to catch. Quite probably giant eels are abnormal; they are fish which have not matured properly and do not experience the spawning urge. It is also possible that eels which have slipped into waters they cannot escape from grow big before they die.

Bream

Tackle: Avon rod. 4–6 lb (1·8–2·7 kg) line.—For snaggy conditions and waters where bream grow as large as double-figures: Carp rod. 7–9 lb (3·1–4 kg) line. Hook sizes 6, 8, 10 and 12.
Hookbait: Bread, cheese, maggots, worms, sausage paste and freshwater mussels.
Groundbait: Large balls of stodge laced with hook samples introduced frequently. Heavy pre-baiting in known hot-spots is advantageous.
Remarks: There are several ways of locating a bream shoal. For a start, the fish roll at the surface prior to feeding, and below where they are last seen is the place to put a hookbait. Faint discoloration of the water also signals bream, rooting pig-like in the mud. Angle upstream of discolorations in moving water.

A location method which bream expert Peter Stone and his friends use is known as the 'cross-over'. It involves several anglers spacing themselves about 10 yd (9 m) apart along the bank. All fish hard for ten minutes and then, if no bream have been caught, the angler furthest upstream moves down

10 yd (9 m) below the end angler and tries again. This system of searching continues at ten-minute intervals until bream are found or the day ends. If bream are located, the anglers muster together as a group to take equal advantage. As bream shoals are often vast there is plenty of fish for everybody.

Spots where bream feed include weirpools, underwater ledges, bulrush beds, areas of submerged lily and deeper holes in shallow lakes. Because bream shoals wander about a great deal, it is possible, in smaller stillwaters, to learn the pattern of their patrol well enough to be able to groundbait an area along the path and halt their progress—at least for as long as groundbait supplies last.

Bream eat enormous quantities of food, and quite honestly it is impossible to over-bait a bream swim. A full sack-load, if it can be carted to the waterside, would certainly not be overdoing things. Once groundbait runs out, the bream move on and you will catch no more. The importance of heavy groundbaiting is as cut and dried as that.

Bream live in many different swims and bite in many different ways. Consequently there is always need to adjust basic float fishing and legering to deal with these changing circumstances. Such techniques as trotting, laying-on, lift-method, stret-pegging, static legering and legering with a lead light enough to sink the bait slowly, are all methods which will be found useful at various times and places.

Should method and bite-pattern allow, the rod can be put in rests with the bale-arm closed. Add a dough-bob or glow-bob as indicator when legering from rests.

Bream feed day and night. In winter, river bream remain active. Those in stillwaters tend to hibernate.

Big Species

Common Carp

Tackle: Carp rod. 8–15 lb (3·6–6·8 kg) line. Size 2, 4, 6 and 8 hooks.
Hookbait: Bread, cheese, freshwater mussels, maggots, sweetcorn, meat baits, potatoes, worms and 'exotics'.
Groundbait: Hook samples thrown or catapulted, and balls of stodge laced with hook samples.
Methods: Freelining and legering.
Remarks: Carp in hard-fished waters have a habit of remaining far out from the bank during the hours of daylight and must be fished for at long range. They are easier to catch after dark because they then move in closer to the bank.

When legering, the rod is put in rests with a silver foil tube indicator; the bale-arm is open. At night the silver foil is replaced with an electric bite alarm. Carp run with the bait, but there is absolutely no reason to let them run very far. As soon as the line is moving, turn in the bale-arm, wait for the line to tighten, and drag, rather than strike,

A carp angler's pitch

the hook home, as the weight of the fish is felt.

In winter it is a good idea to scale the size of bait right down, and to strike at twitch bites. Twitch bites are quick jerks of the indicator caused by carp sucking in and blowing out the bait quickly. Carp often play with baits in this manner when the water is cold.

To hit twitches the bale-arm is closed and a dough-bob or glow-bob indicator is hung about 6 in (15 cm) beneath the rod. Strike fast the moment the indicator moves. An important point is to set the reel to backwind—just in case a carp does charge off with the bait fast. Should this happen with the reel in anti-reverse, either the rod will finish up in the water, or the line will snap.

Twitch bites, of course, also result from little fish nibbling at the bait and bigger fish brushing past the line. The only way to discover the difference is to strike at them.

Carp are often twitch-biters in over-fished public fisheries, no matter what the water temperature is. They also shy away from ordinary baits, and this in turn has lead to the invention of what are collectively called 'exotic baits'—baits concocted from ingredients completely different from those commonly used on the hook. Successful carpmen keep their bait recipes secret for one *very good* reason; once they become general knowledge, used by everybody, they cease to be 'different' and no longer catch carp so effectively.

Exotics are invented by experimenting with edible ingredients which it is thought might appeal to carp, and trying out the resulting 'mixes' to see how the fish respond to them. Plenty of free samples should be introduced to the water as part of these trials. Tinned cat and dog foods are often used in 'something new' carp baits.

Pike

Tackle: Pike rod. 8–15 lb (3·6–6·8 kg) line. Wire traces fitted with treble hooks.—For long-casting herring and mackerel baits: Beachcaster. 15–18 lb (6·8–8·1 kg) line. Side-cast reel.
Hookbait: Fish.
Groundbait: Fish chunks and balls of groundbait mashed with herrings and scented with fish oils.
Methods: Freelining, legering, float fishing and paternostering. Lure fishing with spinners, spoons, plugs and moving deadbaits.

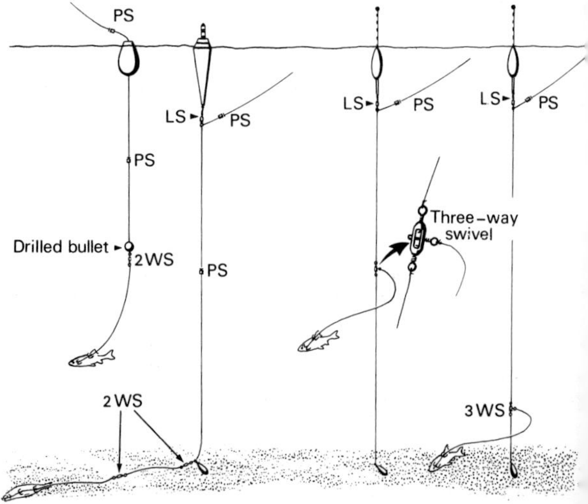

The illustration shows float rigs for pike fishing. The one on the left is ideal for trotting live and dead baits in rivers. Next to it is a deadbait rig for stillwater work which features a self-cocking float. On the right are two paternoster rigs. By comparing them it will be seen that by varying the length of line between the leger lead and the three-way swivel it is possible to fish the livebait at any depth between near-surface and bottom.

The paternoster rig is suitable for both stillwater and river fishing in any swim where it is desirable to restrict the bait's movement to a small area such as a clear hole in an otherwise snaggy section of water. PS = plug-stop, LS = link-swivel, 2WS = two-way swivel, 3WS = three-way swivel.

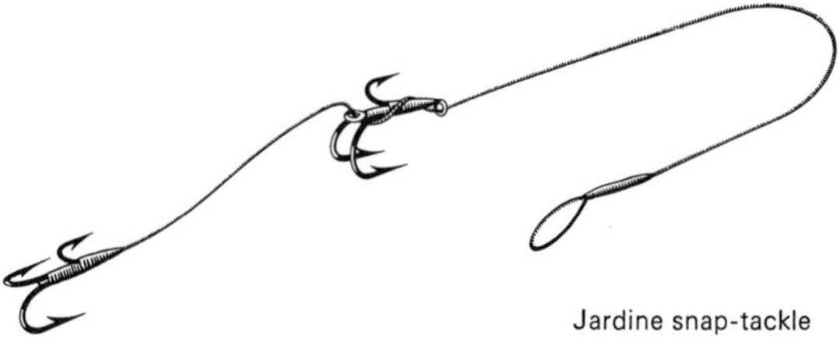

Jardine snap-tackle

The Jardine snap-tackle livebait rig is attached by sticking the small hook on the end treble just astern of the gill cover of the bait and the small hook of the top treble through the leading root of the dorsal fin. The top treble is adjustable along the wire to accommodate baits of different shapes and sizes. Between the main line and the snap-tackle a wire trace is added, attached by a link-swivel to the wire-loop.

Remarks: Pike are extremely fit and lively during summer, and from a purely sporting point of view it is my opinion that lure methods are preferable to bait fish methods at this time of year. Summer pike are everywhere in the water, and hunting systemat-

The author with a brace of big pike weighing 20 lb 4 oz (9.1 kg) and 17 lb 8 oz (7.8 kg), taken in February

ically with lures is a deeply satisfying way of finding them out.

From autumn to the season's end, although pike still respond to lures, bait fish methods come into their own for catching pike of larger size. Every method has its day, but I am firmly convinced that freelining herring and mackerel baits in stillwaters of shallow depth is the number one approach if you want to connect a pike of 20 lb (9 kg) plus.

By the time the season is beginning to draw to a close, pike will already be gathering in groups as preparation for entering the spawning areas. Some groups consist almost entirely of females [the majority of pike weighing upwards of 10 lb (4·5 kg) are females] and if such a group as this can be marked down it is possible to catch a number of specimens between 10 (4·5 kg) and 30 lb (13·6 kg) plus in the space of just a few weeks.

Isolated slacks along stretches of fast-flowing rivers are places to try for big-pike groups. In stillwaters the groups are not so easily located because they roam about quite a bit. The effort is still worth while nevertheless.

I remember a friend of mine visiting a gravel-pit regularly for several winters without even one big pike falling to his rod. Then he stumbled on an in-form hot-spot where his first three runs to deadbaits yielded two pike of over 20 lb (9 kg) each, inside the space of half-a-day's fishing!

Catfish

Tackle: Beachcaster. 15–30 lb (6·8–13·6 kg) line. Wire traces fitted with single hooks.
Hookbaits: Worms and small fish.
Groundbait: Balls of groundbait mashed with herrings and fish oils.
Methods: Legering and freelining.
Remarks: Because catfish are so rare in this country very little is known about them. It is known, however, that they reach enormous size in the lakes at Woburn Abbey, and that they pack tremendous strength.

Angling for catfish is undertaken with the rod in rests and the bale-arm open. One of the major problems is getting a firm hook-hold. Catfish often fail to take the bait properly and missed runs are a consequence. The strike should be delayed as long as possible.

Catfish are warm water feeders, only ever likely to be caught when the temperature rises above 60°F (15°C).

Lighter strength tackle, a carp rod and 10 lb (4·5 kg) line, is adequate for dealing with small catfish in open water, but such gear could never be expected to subdue monster 'cats'—fish weighing as much as 60 (27·2) to 80 lb (36·2 kg).

Handling Fish

Playing

Small fish are easily and quickly brought under control by applying gentle rod pressure and turning the handle of the reel. The only point which must be watched for is that a fish does not come to the surface and flap about—disturbance capable of scaring off the remainder of the shoal. This activity can be avoided by keeping the rod top low towards the water and winding back slowly.

Big fish, and the bigger and tougher they are the more this applies, must be 'played' long enough to tire them before any attempt is made to lift them out. Exactly how an individual fish is played depends largely on the type of swim where it is hooked. If a fish is hooked amid thick weed or close to snags, quite obviously it cannot be allowed much line at any time during the fight. Clearly this is the reason why strong rods, lines and hooks are required when fishing such parts as lily 'jungles'.

In open water, lighter tackle can be used and the fish allowed to exhaust itself by running against rod pressure; the slipping-clutch of the fixed-spool reel is set tight enough to give line only in the event that the fish tugs extra hard or puts on a sudden burst of speed.

The fighting habits of fish vary from one species to the next but, broadly speaking, they consist of strong runs interspaced with lulls, when the fish moves more slowly or allows itself to be brought in close to the bank.

As examples, I will outline the typical fight patterns of two of the strongest species in fresh water—barbel and carp.

First barbel: We will imagine that a 6 lb (2·7 kg) class barbel has been hooked 10 yd (9 m) downstream in fastish water. Immediately it will feel heavy as it thumps against the arched rod, and inevitably your heart starts to quicken its beat. This is the very time to remain calm to resist the impulse to pull hard on the rod and try to drag the fish in. At this stage, too great a pressure will send the barbel off on a mad run downstream, forcing you to run also to keep up with it—if it hasn't broken free of course!

Steady pressure is what is wanted. Enough to keep the fish moving and sapping energy, but no

Downstream pressure is applied as the barbel fights upstream of the angler

more than that. With luck the fish will fin upstream, going above the spot on the bank where you are standing. This manoeuvre is favourable because downstream pressure can then be applied to coax the fish to fight both the rod and the current. This action serves to exhaust it, so that when eventually it does fall back it will be tired—perhaps even ready for the net. Should the barbel remain downstream, walk down the bank, keeping contact by taking in line as you go, and get well below the fish that way.

The fight from a barbel of this size may last minutes or for as long as a quarter of an hour. There will be quiet periods when the fish pushes against the current neither giving nor taking line, other times when it will be brought almost as far as the net, and crucial moments which leave you weak at the knees when panic moves send line screaming from the reel.

Played out and on its side, the barbel is ready for the net

Keep patient, keep cool, and above all try to be always downstream of the fish. Eventually, after what will almost certainly seem an eternity, the barbel will tumble on to its flank and be ready for netting.

Two developments to beware of: (1) A barbel which allows itself to be brought straight to the bank after being hooked. *Watch out for a long run.* The fish could be either big or foul-hooked in a fin; not realizing at first that anything is wrong. If you do get a run of this kind, do not try to stop it too abruptly or you will part the line for sure. (2) A barbel which is exhausted, but gives one last dash to the centre of the river just as you are about to net it out. An exhausted barbel on a long line can be a difficult customer because it no longer has the ability to resist the current properly. Gradually it drags off downstream, and if you do not react fast, run after it and pressure it back to the bank, you could be in real trouble.

Patience is a virtue when playing barbel. A double-figure specimen can take as long as an hour to beat even on correct strength tackle. In my opinion, if you can handle barbel you can handle any fish in the river. They do not come any stronger than this species.

Now carp. This time the fish is a ten-pounder (4·5 kg), hooked in a lake swim where a patch of lilies grows to the right and a fallen tree rests in the water to the left. The strike has been made, and after a second or two to think about it the fish has powered off hard and fast straight out from the bank towards open water. No snags or thick weed to worry about so the fish can be let run against medium pressure. Eventually it slows up, and by pumping the rod—lifting and lowering it and winding in line on the downward strokes—you find it can

(*above*) A swirl, and the carp makes off on a second run

(*below*) Steady pumping brings the carp closer and closer

be brought grudgingly back towards the bank. Occasionally the slipping-clutch grates a yard or two of line as the fish shakes its head, but otherwise it is a time to breathe deeply and calm down (an angler would not be an angler if he didn't shake a bit when he hooks a good fish!).

Just as you are beginning to wonder if the carp has had enough, it suddenly wakes up and off it goes again on a second run; this time it moves more to the left and not so far. You start to pump the rod, but the resistance is more stubborn. The fish, in fact, has started to 'kite'—turning broadside on to where you are standing and using the depth of its body to cruise towards the fallen tree. Now there *is* cause for concern. If the fish reaches the tree it will cut the line the moment it makes contact with the rough bark.

Straightaway the rod is swung parallel to the bank pointing away from the tree and sidestrain is applied to as much as the tackle will stand. At first it has no result, the fish keeps on course towards the tree. But then, as the greater pressure begins to drag it off balance it veers round and starts coming back to the bank yet again.

Steady pumping brings it closer and closer. A few short runs are counteracted without trouble. Then it sees the approaching net, senses acute danger and crashes off with all its remaining strength towards the lilies. Sidestrain is applied in the opposite direction, and though the fish does enter the stems a little way the taut line rips through the foliage and it is soon free again—this time flopped on its side as a truly beaten fish.

Summing up: Let a big stillwater fish run if it has a mind to, and the area it is in is snagless. Apply sidestrain when the situation looks dangerous. Retrieve line by pumping. Never attempt to wind line back against a running fish to stop it—rather finger the edge of the drum to slow it up. And above all, stay calm.

Netting

Very small fish can be taken from the water by swinging them out on the line. When doing this it is essential to have enough line between rod-tip and fish to allow the fish to come back into the hand.

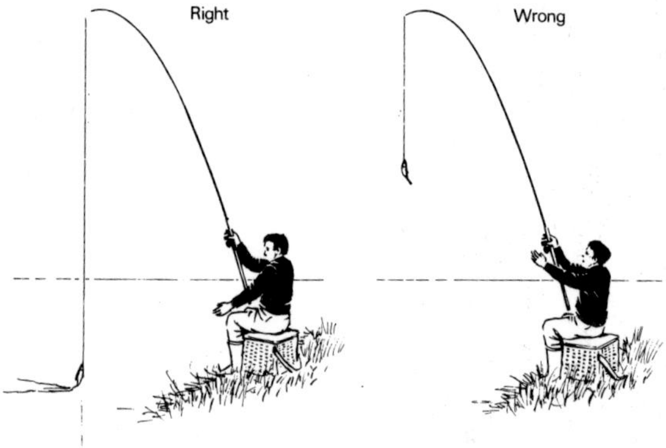

Swinging a small fish out on the line

Fish heavier than about half-a-pound (226 g) should be netted. To net a fish, the landing net is submerged deeply and the fish drawn over the rim. The net is then lifted to engulf the fish inside the mesh. By remaining seated the angler is less likely to frighten other fish which might be feeding in the swim.

Never attempt to put the net under the fish. Always bring the fish over the net. To get a big

Netting a fish

fish from water to bank, first make sure it is fully enclosed, then lay the rod down, and grip frame and mesh with both hands for lifting out. It is helpful when handling an exceptionally big fish to have a friend take care of the netting for you—but be absolutely sure he understands the procedure, and does not attempt to lift the net until he is told to do so. This is vitally important to avoid completely any confusion which might arise. The rule is that the man with the rod controls the man with the net.

Unhooking

Handle fish with wet hands or with a damp cloth when unhooking them. If the hook is so far back

Artery forceps being used to unhook a small roach

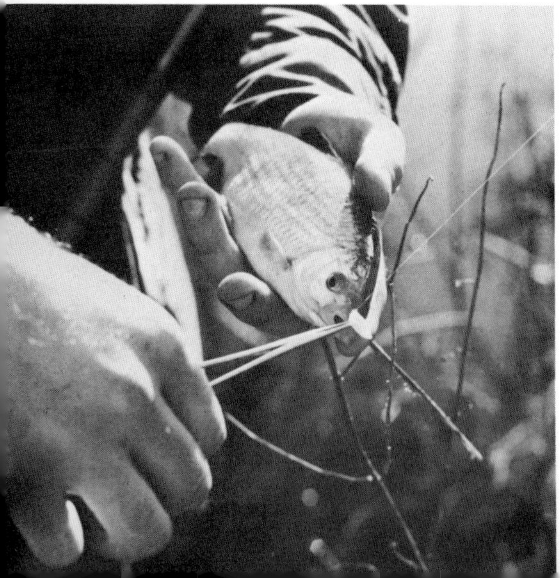

that it cannot be retrieved with the fingers the best tool to use is a pair of artery forceps.

To unhook pike and zander special tools are required: a selection of mouth gags of various sizes (points taped over to avoid undue injury); a pair of pliers and a pair of end-snips fitted with long handles; and a model-maker's knife blade also mounted on a long handle.

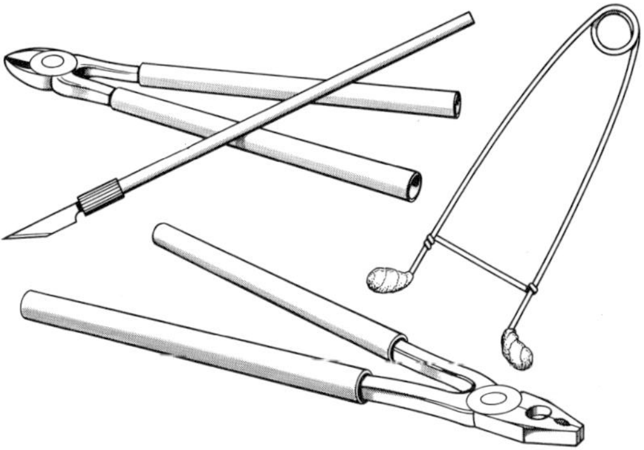

Unhooking tools

First pull the pike clear of the netting and, if it is large, wrap it in a wet sack or old bath towel. Hold the body of the pike still, and insert as small a gag as possible to open its mouth wide. The hooks, even when quite far back, can be removed with the pliers. If you sit on the ground by the pike, you can control its movements with your own body and work really close in without fear of getting bitten. Care must be taken not to damage the fish by applying too much pressure.

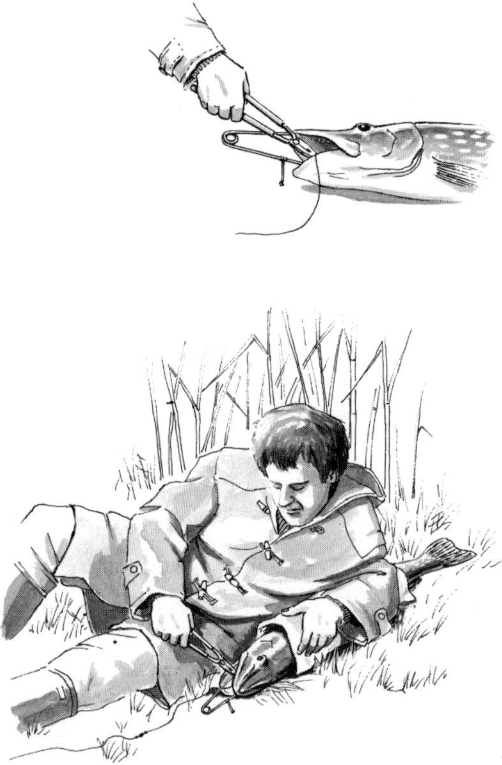

Unhooking a pike

The knife blade sometimes helps when it is necessary to remove a hook nicked in loose skin, but if the hooks are so far back that they cannot be seen at all it is advisable to cut through the wire with the snips as far down the throat as possible.

An important aspect of piking, which quite honestly I cannot emphasize enough, is *never* to purposely delay the strike so long that a pike has time to swallow the hooks down to the stomach.

Handlifting a pike

Far better to strike early and risk missing a secure hook-hold, than gut-hook and sentence a fine, sporting fish to an early death.

Incidentally, it is not absolutely necessary to use a net to land small pike and zander. A fish of either species as large as 10 lb (4·5 kg) can be removed from the water by gripping it with one hand firmly across the back, astern of the gill-covers, and hoisting it out.

Photographing

Photographing the catch is the ideal way to preserve a permanent record of notable specimens and memorable bags. *For the sake of the fish it must be carried out carefully.* Don't keep fish out of water longer than absolutely necessary. Don't let them flap about on dry ground. Don't squeeze them tight or hug them against rough clothing. Don't hold them at peculiar angles which could damage their vital organs (e.g. upside down).

The most sensible plan is to have the camera ready for instant use all the time. This means that as soon as a big fish is unhooked it can be photographed and slipped back into water in a very short space of time.

Before sliding out a bag of fish for photographing, soak the area (short soft grass for preference) and keep a bucket of water on hand to wash the fish over with. It takes time to put (say) a couple of dozen dace back in the water and some of the fish left until last can dry out if the day is hot. *Never throw fish back.*

Weighing

Catches of fish are best weighed still in the keepnet. After the fish have been let free the keepnet is then weighed again and its weight is deducted to get the accurate weight of the fish.

A big crucian carp weighed accurately in a plastic bag on dial-clock scales

Big fish can be weighed individually in a thick plastic bag or soft-mesh bag, subtracting the weight of the container afterwards, of course.

Spring-balance scales and dial-clock scales are used to weigh fish. The latter type is more accurate and also adjustable so that the weight of the container can be compensated before weighing the catch.

Retaining and Returning

For various reasons it is necessary to retain fish for a period following capture before returning them in good condition.

Hard-fighters such as barbel and tench benefit greatly from being rested in a keepnet to recover strength and balance, particularly when they are going to be returned to a river of strong current. I have seen, for example, barbel floating belly-up and slowly dying, not because they were injured, but

Ron Barnett gently returns a fine 12 lb (5·4 kg) carp caught by the author

because they had been released too soon to be able to combat the swift-flowing current.

Notable specimens caught at night must also be retained in order to photograph them properly on the morning after. True, it is possible to picture fish in the dark, but it is never an easy exercise. It takes a lot of fiddling about and adjusting this and that. And if you want to use a flash gun without scaring other fish in the swim and annoying fellow anglers, it calls for a long walk away from the water carrying both camera gear and the trophy fish.

Returning a fish

Clearly it is essential for matchmen to keep what they land, and it is equally clear that in certain circumstances when pleasure fishing it can spoil the swim to return caught fish among those which are still to be caught.

Keepnets should be of large size, staked out along the bottom so that fish have plenty of room to move and change position. Wide-mesh knotted keepnets are a menace because the roughness of the knots removes scales and protective slime and the width of the mesh causes fin-split. Such injuries can lead to the death of the victims—perhaps even the spread of disease to other fish and a resulting widespread fatality.

In recent years a new type of keepnet has been introduced to the market made from knotless micro-mesh material. Extensive testing has proved how superior these nets are for preserving fish in perfect order. This is the only type I would personally recommend.

If a big fish is to be returned straight to the water it should be handled with extreme care; hold it between the hands on an even keel until it is able to wiggle clear. Stroking the flanks lightly helps aid recovery. When returning a big fish to a river it is vital to hold it with its head pointing upstream directly into the current. If a fish is held with its head pointing downstream for any length of time it will die.

Carp anglers successfully retain their big fish caught at night in loose-weave potato sacks—one fish per sack.

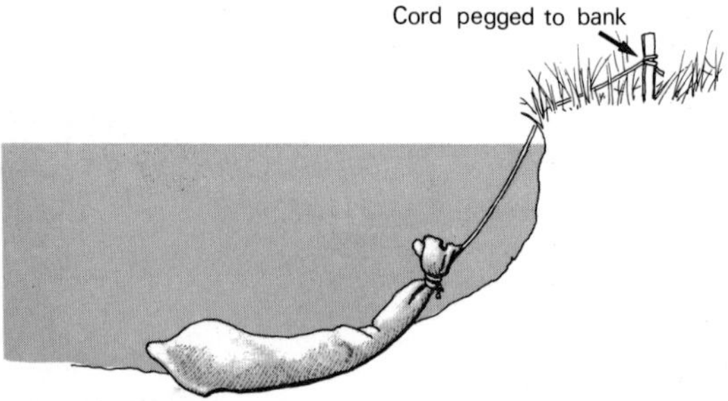

The sack method of retaining carp individually

4: FINAL MATTERS

Sporting Divisions

Coarse fish are hunted for the pleasure and interest which comes from trying to catch them, and for the feelings of excitement and satisfaction which follow whenever the attempt is successful. Few of the coarse species have any real value at table; even the edible ones are very little eaten apart from eels. Coarse fishing is really just a 'catch and return' activity, and few are those who purposely seek coarse fish to eat.

It goes without saying that coarse fishing is fun for everybody who participates but, in the jargon of the angler, the term 'fun fishing' takes on special meaning; it describes the activities of non-specialists—the vast ranks of those who simply go fishing for the balm of catching a few fish and 'getting away from it all'.

Personally, I think this is what fishing is really all about and the way to enjoy it. It does not necessarily follow, of course, that the knowledge and ability of 'fun fishers' has to remain limited. Through practical angling, observation, and a study of thoughts and ideas expressed by fellow anglers in books and articles, it is possible to become proficient to the point where, providing they are in the water, specimen fish can be caught in return for little increased effort.

Many friends of mine have long lists of notable catches to their credit, yet strongly deny they are anything but 'fun fishers'. They know the basics of the sport well enough to take advantage of every opportunity which comes their way, but that is as far as their 'specimen hunting' inclinations go.

'Specimen hunting' is a significant division of coarse fishing—highly specialized these days. Some specimen hunters are happy to seek big fish of all species, according to season and what big-fish water they can obtain access to. Other specimen hunters specialize in just one or two species; they learn everything they can about the habits of their chosen quarry and strive always to improve tackle, methods and baits to catch them with.

The pinnacle of achievement for many specimen hunters is the breaking of a British record. Yet, ironically, few indeed are records topped by fish caught by anglers who, at time of capture, confidently thought themselves in with a chance of beating the best for a certain species.

To increase knowledge of big fish and big fish waters, specimen hunters band together in groups—both locally and nationally. Many of these groups form a larger organization known as the National Association of Specimen Groups.

In addition to groups the N.A.S.G. is now also open to individual members and independent angling clubs. For details contact the president, G. E. Hodson, 45 Long Croft Road, Dronfield Woodhouse, Sheffield, S18 5XU.

Famous national single-species groups—with memberships including both specimen hunters and non-specimen hunters of proven ability—include The Tenchfishers', The Barbel Catchers' Club, The National Anguilla Club (eels), and the British Carp Study Group. The latter group is by far the most advanced in the country, printing its own magazine, *The Carp*, and operating a special advisory service to answer the carp fishing problems of non-members. This service is open to all, and requests for information should be addressed to the secretary, Peter Mohan, Heywood House, Pill, Bristol. BS20 0AE.

Mr Mohan is also secretary of the Carp Anglers Association, an organization open to all who are interested in carp fishing—even those who have still to catch their first carp. There are two divisions of membership—senior and junior—with the junior section limited to under 16's.

Another excellent single-species group is the Pike Anglers' Club, with a membership divided into senior members (highly experienced pike anglers) and associate members (less experienced anglers including beginners and youngsters). It, too, publishes its own magazine. For further information contact the secretary, Barrie Rickards, 4 Willow Crescent, Milton, Cambridgeshire.

Specimen hunting is a first-class approach for really keen anglers. But be warned, do not let the hunt for bigger and bigger fish get out of hand. It is so easy to become dissatisfied with results if they fall short of expectations, and the result is that the enjoyment of 'going fishing' ceases to have meaning.

There is a true story of one specimen hunter who dearly wanted to catch a 20 lb (9 kg) carp. He tried very hard for several years, with tackle and methods unquestionably excellent, and because of his ability he landed a high total of carp weighing between 10 lb (4·5 kg) and 19 lb 12 oz (8·9 kg). The 20 lb (9 kg) target eluded him though, and eventually a matter of 4 oz (113 g) caused him to suffer a nervous breakdown.

The moral, if you fancy taking up specimen hunting after learning the ropes for a few seasons, is to set your sights high by all means, but never to forget that small fish are worth catching too. Enjoy the fun of small fish and the big fish will follow—without any loss of mental health!

'Match fishing' is a third division of coarse angling. Matches are fished as individual events and team events, in leagues and as annual championships. Most matches are 'pegged down' with each participant restricted to a single spot on the bank by drawing a ticket with a number on it corresponding to the number on a peg stuck in the ground at that spot. Less frequently matches are fished as 'rovers', allowing those taking part to select their own swims by going off, one from each team at few minute intervals. In winter, 'fur and feather' matches take place, sometimes solely for pike. Boxing Day is a popular date for these contests.

Years ago match winners received a copper or brass kettle, or other metal ornament as prize, and it was easy to judge how good a particular matchman was from the amount of 'shine' in his front parlour.

Modern match fishing is quite different. Major fixtures are sponsored with big-money prize lists, and top matchmen put a lot of behind-the-scenes effort into winning important events. Match 'stars' often speak of a season's success in terms of money won rather than in terms of good fish and notable catches. It is not everybody's idea of what angling should be about, but nevertheless, for those who find pleasure in competing against fellow anglers as well as against fish, match fishing is *the* sporting division with greatest appeal.

Fly Fishing

There has not been space in this book to deal with fly fishing. Special rods and lines are required, and the casting style is quite separate from all other forms of casting. Coarse fish caught with fly tackle and imitations of insects and fish constructed from fur, feather and silk, include rudd, dace, chub, grayling, bleak, pike, barbel, carp and perch. Further information is contained in my book *The Observer's Book of Fly Fishing* (Warne).

Lines and Baited Hooks Kill

Nylon monofilament fishing line has a habit of losing its strength, and as some anglers know to their cost a big fish hooked on last year's line is often lost in the first moment that pressure is applied. On the other hand, nylon line does not rot, and though it may deteriorate, becoming as weak as cotton, it still remains strong enough to kill birds and animals which become entwined in it.

Sad pictures of birds are published which prove just how fatal fishing line is to wildlife; pictures depict robins and finches hanging by their legs from monofilament tangled in tree branches, and blackbirds and thrushes strangled in their undergrowth homes.

But not only the smaller birds. A goosander drake, reported in a past issue of *Birds*, the magazine of the Royal Society for the Protection of Birds, apparently died in the agony of total starvation with its beak clamped tight by a chunk of monofilament no longer than 5 ft (1·5 m).

Angling is getting a bad name because of the menace of unwanted line left unthinkingly along the bank, and it is a stigma which can only be removed by practical action: *take home every piece of waste line and burn it.*

In awkward casting spots, trees are decorated with hooks, spinners, floats and nylon lengths, and these also should be removed if at all possible.

Another kind of monofilament menace is created by anglers who will insist on fishing fine lines in snaggy water for big-growing species. Apart from the fact that beating a heavy carp or barbel from a lily-bed or thick streamer weed on light gear is very much a trust-to-luck affair, it also means that when breaks occur (they often do) long trails of line are left threaded through the growth—definite traps for coots, moorhens, swans and ducks, as they paddle about up-tailing to feed on the weed.

Baited hooks out of the water are killers, too. Anglers leaving swims for any length of time should wind their tackle in and clean the hook of bait. After all, a bunch of maggots is an open invitation to a friendly robin, a crust to a swan, half a sausage to a dog or cat. Such incidents really do happen, believe me!

★ ★ ★

The Anglers' Co-operative Association

This organization was founded in 1948 by angler and barrister John Eastwood, KC. It is a voluntary body and its aim is to fight water pollution through the common law, the legal and administrative costs being shared by anglers and others interested in the conservation of rivers and lakes and the fish they contain. Apart from membership subscriptions it has no other means of support.

Since its formation the ACA has fought over 1,000 serious cases of pollution, losing only one and that merely because of a technicality.

Not all anglers are members but all anglers should be. The ACA is the most successful safeguard we have in the constant battle against those who thoughtlessly and carelessly defile precious water. A membership of over 10,000, including 1,000 angling clubs and associations, believes this to be true.

For further information write to the ACA, Midland Bank Chambers, Westgate, Grantham, Lincs. NG31 6LE. Currently the ACA handles over fifty cases of pollution at any one time. That kind of action takes money—your money. A year's subscription to the ACA costs less than the price of ticket and bait for a decent day's fishing, so there is no excuse for not giving this organization the support it deserves.

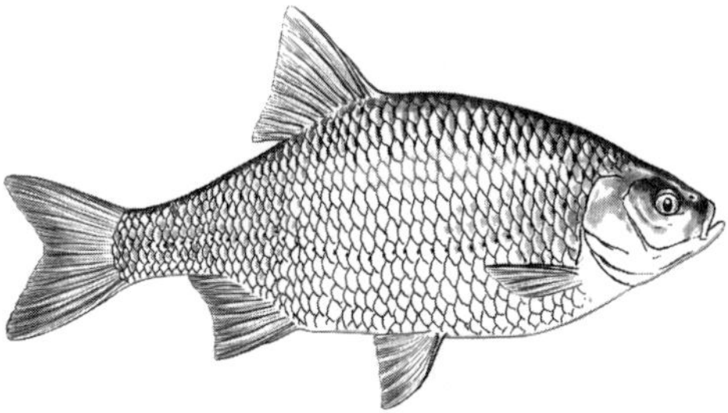

Size of Fish in British Waters

Species	*Quality*	*Specimen*	*Possible Maximum Size*
Roach	1 lb (·45 kg)	2 lb (·9 kg)	4½–5 lb (2–2·2 kg)
Rudd (England)	1 lb (·45 kg)	2 lb (·9 kg)	5 lb (2·2 kg)
Rudd (Ireland)	1½ lb (·68 kg)	2½ lb (1·1 kg)	5 lb (2·2 kg)
Dace	6–8 oz (170–226 g)	12 oz (340 g)	1½–1¾ lb (·68–·79 kg)
Crucian Carp	1 lb (·45 kg)	2 lb (·9 kg)	6–6½ lb (2·7–2·9 kg)
Common Carp (Wild)	4 lb (1·8 kg)	10 lb (4·5 kg)	20 lb (9 kg)
Common Carp (King)	8 lb (3·6 kg)	20 lb (9 kg)	60–70 lb (27·2–31·7 kg)
Common Bream	4 lb (1.8 kg)	10 lb (4·5 kg)	16 lb (7·2 kg)
Silver Bream	8 oz (226 g)	1½ lb (·68 kg)	4 lb (1·8 kg)
Chub	3 lb (1·3 kg)	5 lb (2·2 kg)	10–12 lb (4·5–5·4 kg)
Tench	3 lb (1·3 kg)	5 lb (2·2 kg)	12–15 lb (5·4—6·8 kg)
Grayling	1 lb (·45 kg)	2 lb (·9 kg)	5 lb (2·2 kg)
Perch	1 lb (·45 kg)	3 lb (1·3 kg)	6–8 lb (2·7–3·6 kg)
Pike (River)	5 lb (2·2 kg)	15 lb (6·8 kg)	40–45 lb (18·1–20·4 kg)
Pike (Stillwater)	8 lb (3·6 kg)	20 lb (9 kg)	70 lb (31·7 kg)
Zander	5 lb (2·2 kg)	10 lb (4·5 kg)	20–25 lb (9–11·3 kg)
Barbel	5 lb (2·2 kg)	10 lb (4·5 kg)	20 lb (9 kg)
Eel	2 lb (·9 kg)	5 lb (2·2 kg)	20 lb+ (9 kg)
Catfish	Not widely enough distributed to offer comparisons		80 lb (36·2 kg)

Books for Further Reading

Catch More Roach and Rudd by James Randell. Wolfe Publishing

Successful Roach Fishing by David Carl Forbes. David & Charles

Catch More Dace by Peter Wheat. Wolfe Publishing

Catch More Carp by Jack Hilton. Wolfe Publishing

Carp For Everyone by Peter Mohan. David & Charles

Quest For Carp by Jack Hilton. Pelham Books

Carp by James A. Gibbinson. Macdonald & Janes

Catch More Bream by Dennis Kelly. Wolfe Publishing

The Complete Chub Angler by Ken Seaman. David & Charles

Catch More Chub by Fred Wagstaffe. Wolfe Publishing

Tench by Fred J. Taylor. Macdonald & Janes

Fishing For Big Tench by Barrie Rickards and Ray Webb. Rod & Gun Publishing

Catch More Tench by Bob Church. Wolfe Publishing

Grayling by Reg Righyni. Macdonald & Janes

Catch More Perch by Barrie Rickards. Wolfe Publishing

Fishing For Big Pike by Ray Webb and Barrie Rickards. Black

Pike by Fred Buller. Macdonald & Janes

Catch More Pike by David Allen. Wolfe Publishing

Pike by Jim Gibbinson. Osprey Publishing

The Fighting Barbel by Peter Wheat. Benn

Catch More Barbel by Ken Cope. Wolfe Publishing

Fishing As We Find It. Peter Wheat (editor). Warne

Catch A Big Fish. David Carl Forbes (editor). Newnes

In Search of Big Fish by Frank Guttfield. EMAP

Match Fishing by Dave Burr and Jack Winstanley. Hamlyn

Match Angling. John Carding (editor) Pan Angler's Library

Match Fishing To Win by Billy Lane and Colin Graham. Macdonald & Janes

Pelham Manual of River Coarse Fishing by Peter Wheat. Pelham Books

Still-Water Angling by Richard Walker. David & Charles

Small Stream Fishing by David Carl Forbes. Newnes

Irish Coarse Fishing by James Williams. Black

Billy Lane's Encyclopaedia of Float Fishing by Billy Lane and Colin Graham. Pelham Books

Rigs and Tackles by Fred Buller. Macdonald & Janes

The New Encyclopaedia of Coarse Fishing Baits by Colin Graham. Macdonald & Janes

Angling and The Law by Michael Gregory. Charles Knight

Where To Fish. Harmsworth Press

Fishing Waters. Compiled by Bill Howes. Link House Group

British Freshwater Fishes by M. E. Varley. Angling News (Books)

Geoffrey Bucknall's Book of Fly-Fishing. Nelson

The Observer's Book of Fly Fishing by Peter Wheat. Warne

Index